D1123447

Roll Away The Stone

SAVING AMERICA'S CHILDREN

What people are saying about

Roll Away The Stone

"The first stone Fred Taylor ever cast was the one that blocked the futures of some wonderful people who happened to be orphan children. And he did not cast that stone at any person; he cast it aside so as to undo the heavy burden. *Roll Away the Stone* will be an American classic. It belongs on the shelf of every unselfish American."

Andy Jacobs Jr.
Former Indiana Congressman

"Fred Taylor has written an unusual book. He does not allow himself to just "understand" the outer face of the poor, marginalized individuals he meets, but to share the revelation they are to him. He finds in biblical metaphor the challenge for social response—and for community."

Sister Mary Paul
Director of Clinical Services
Center for Family Life in Sunset Park
Brooklyn, NY

"*In Roll Away the Stone,* Fred Taylor demonstrates a new paradigm for the new millennium: religious and other communities, individuals, and families reaching out to one another with love and trust to resurrect those for whom hope is dead. This fine book shows the way."

Marian Wright Edelman
President,
The Children's Defense Fund

"In this remarkable book Taylor draws on his deep spiritual roots and 30 years of work with families and on the streets of Washington, DC to illuminate how much work can be done to change the lives of children who are 'hidden from public view,' growing up with no realistic possibility of a decent life."

Lisbeth Schorr
Author of "Common Purpose"

"This is an important book! It pulls together elements of opportunity for breakthrough in economics, politics, and down home neighborhood development in ways that can surely point the way."

Joan McKinney
Executive Director
Center for Creative Visioning

"All of us who are ground down by the daily struggle against seemingly intractable social problems need to hear Fred Taylor's message of hope. Fred uses the story of his own agency's birth and its 30-year evolution to show that progress is possible —and to itemize what it takes. Then he zooms out from FLOC's history to the future to suggest some exciting new directions for our progress as a species."

David S. Liederman
Executive Director
Child Welfare League of America

Roll Away The Stone

SAVING AMERICA'S CHILDREN

by
Fred Taylor

Foreword by
Lisbeth Schorr

Roll Away The Stone

Publisher: Information International
Copyright 1999, Fred Taylor

Library of Congress Cataloging-in-Publication

Taylor, Fred, 1932-
    Roll away the stone: saving America's children / by Fred Taylor. -- 1st ed.
      p. cm.
      Includes bibliographical references.
      Preassigned LCCN: 98-71938
      ISBN: 1-882480-46-5

      1. Child welfare--United States--Religious aspects. 2. Church work with the poor.   3. Church work with children.   I. Title.

BV639.P6T39 1999   261.8'3271
                             QBI98-1094

Printed in the United States of America

Dedication

To my father, Rumsey Barnes Taylor, 1902-98, able businessman, churchman, political activist, community leader, champion of youth, and a superb mentor. With deep respect and appreciation.

Table of Contents

Acknowledgments

This book started ten years ago when my friend Mary Clare Powell, who had written the FLOC newsletter for several years, said to me, "Fred, there's a book in the FLOC experience and you're the one to write it." I demurred, "But I'm not a writer." She replied, "You will learn, and I'll help you." She then sat me down in front of a tape recorder and interviewed me several times, each time typing up my thoughts with instructions to start writing from the notes. I started producing fragments to which she gave encouraging feedback. The metaphor of the Lazarus story emerged as a framework, and I was off and running. Mary Clare subsequently moved to another city, and we kept the process going by correspondence.

I got so far and realized I needed a larger context. In 1987, I met Drexel Sprecher, developer of the American Renaissance leadership training programs, took his fascinating week long seminar "The Future of Leadership," and picked up my writing project again, with Drexel giving generous feedback and suggestions. Marjorie Suchocki and Bill Lewis did the same. Others who helped along the way include John Anderson, Terry Colvin, Muriel Lipp,

Ryland Swain, John Manwell, Jerry Rardin, Ron Pasquariello, Marc Anderson, Tom Cunningham, Martha Simpson, Sybil Wolin, Rolfe Nordlie and Bill Slack. Their support and encouragement helped greatly.

Next I came to know Mary Liepold, a very talented editor of the Child Welfare League of America, now director of program resources, who graciously edited the entire manuscript (inspiring me and helping me improve my writing in the process). Finally, my friend Mark Cooper put me in touch with publisher Bob Sullivan whose warm personality and astute professionalism have made the final step of publication actually fun. The icing on the cake was Lisbeth Schorr's immediate and enthusiastic acceptance of my request to write the Foreword.

The Forum and other courses provided by the Landmark Education Corporation were particularly valuable and vital resources of validation, clarification and encouragement for my work and producing this book.

Lastly, I want to convey my heartfelt thanks to my wife, Sherrill, who is a social worker and fellow child advocate, to the hundreds of supportive volunteers, staff, and board members over the years at FLOC, the children and families we have served who have met us more than halfway, and gifted child advocate colleagues in Washington, DC and across the country with whom I share a common passion. Together we comprise a powerful community of concern and action, and I pray that this book will advance true empowerment for all children and their families.

Foreword

by Lisbeth Schorr
Author of
*Common Purpose: Strengthening Families
and Neighborhoods to Rebuild America*

Roll Away the Stone is a spiritual call-to-arms and a front-line report from the battlefield. Fred Taylor is one of the small band who have not given up on social change, and offers us an antidote to despair.

In this remarkable book, the Reverend Fred Taylor, Baptist missionary to the poor, draws on his deep spiritual roots and his 30 years of work with families and on the streets of Washington, DC to illuminate how much can be done to change the lives of the children who are "hidden from public view, growing up with no realistic possibility of a decent life." Although he confesses that the worsening situation of children in the nation's capital—and indeed the nation as a whole— often pushes him to the brink of despair, he has assigned himself the task of helping all of us to get unstuck from resignation, disbelief, and cynicism, to enable us to find common ground, and "to uncover the dimension of hope and possibility."

Roll Away the Stone takes us beyond the polarizing debate between liberals and conservatives, and sterile either/or choices, addressing people of all social classes and all ideological persuasions who want to live in a more decent society. Taylor maintains that we do not have to reconcile ourselves to living surrounded by homelessness, deprivation, child abuse, a growing social underclass, or an ever-widening gap between the rich and the poor. He refutes the myth that the world is too complex and too evil for the average citizen to be able to accomplish anything at the community or societal level.

In calling on us to move from cynicism to possibility, he asks us to imagine a community that works for everyone, a community not fragmented by special interests working at cross purposes, where the privileged enjoy their comforts and try to contain—in prisons and in the inner city—those that threaten those comforts. He asks how the connection can be restored among all Americans, including the 10 percent of the population living out their lives in brutal isolation from the rest of the society.

Taylor's message of hope is solidly based in real-world, grass roots experience. He was a Baptist pastor in Suburban Washington in 1965 when a group of Washington area ministers returned from demonstrations in Selma, Alabama, against racial segregation in the South, determined to change unacceptable conditions in their own community. They were particularly concerned about the misguided use of large institutions to warehouse homeless, abused, and neglected children. A single large institution, Junior

Village, housed nearly a thousand such children at the time the ministers focused public attention on what the Washington Post termed "a factory for mental illness."

Taylor helped to create For Love of Children (FLOC), an unusually effective coalition among churches, child advocates, and concerned citizens to create better ways of caring for the city's children. The coalition was determined to end the harm being done at Junior Village, where too many children whose families could have cared for them with a little help were being held, and where those already traumatized by separation from home, family, and neighborhood received none of the nurturance they so urgently required.

In 1966, FLOC raised $10,000, which allowed the new organization to hire Taylor, then 34 years old and a FLOC volunteer, as its first—and to this date only full-time director. FLOC at that point defined its mission as combining advocacy with support of the day-to-day struggle to raise foster children. It recruited, trained, and supported foster parents, while also developing recommendations for an alternative foster care system for the District of Columbia.

Working in partnership with the District's Department of Public Welfare to implement an emergency financial assistance and shelter program, FLOC participated in reducing the population confined at Junior Village from 900 to 600 in a single year. The numbers fell further as FLOC and other agencies recruited new families to become foster parents, opened well-staffed group homes, found housing for families whose children would otherwise have been removed from home, and put pressure on the system from outside to become more responsive to the needs of both children and families. FLOC worked with church-based and ecumenical groups to create foster homes where a married couple or two women would care for groups of children, including some with special needs, generating more than 100 such foster placements in four years.

In its efforts to reduce the number of children in the system, as well as the time they spend in the system, to support families to stay together, and to assure good care for children in the system, FLOC acted very strategically. It was able to attract *The Washington Post's* attention to the conditions at Junior Village, and to project an alternative vision: a home for every child, a home in which every child would be raised with compassion in a family whose basic needs were met. This vision, Taylor writes, was "specific enough to be compelling and large enough to stretch people's hearts." People responded because "the vision called out the best in them—their highest values, their most compassionate and altruistic impulses."

And Junior Village was finally closed—not because of a single action or a single person, Taylor believes, but because of a convergence of energy, persistence, and people coming together around the vision.

FLOC organized its work around an explicit philosophy of high trust and low control—volunteers and staff were given significant responsibility and the authority to act. FLOC was not just well-meaning, but always well-informed. "We had done our homework, and we did it consistently, over and over."

FLOC was small enough and strategic enough to be able to operate pragmatically, responding to needs as they surfaced. When the coalition discovered that inner city schools had so many children with special needs that children had to act out in dramatic ways to get special help, it hired an educational specialist to monitor school progress of all the children in FLOC family foster homes. Similarly, when it turned out that alienated African American adolescents were not faring well in most foster care placements, FLOC established a therapeutic group home for ten adolescent boys.

Taylor describes the struggles of these youngsters. They want to "be somebody," to gain respect—even while they are poor achievers in school, give up easily when frustrated, have poor control over their impulses, and resort to inflicting pain when angry. He lets the reader in on how the director of FLOC's group home is able to deal with these young men whose lives are a perpetual con game, a power struggle with adult authority figures. The director makes clear that the staff are in charge; the staff are able to convey that they care enough and are strong enough to take care of their charges. The environment is one of order, discipline, high expectations, and encouragement so that the youngsters can concentrate on intellectual tasks. The adults never relinquish the role of the adult, however provoked.

Thirty years of work in the trenches with FLOC, as well as his own studies and religious training, form the foundations of Fred Taylor's wise proposals for the future.

First, he asks us to avoid being doctrinaire and simplistic in our effort to understand the causes of the problem.

While our national myth says that anyone, no matter how humble in origin, can make it in America, this is not the case for a significant segment of Americans. These are the children, women and men who exist outside the mainstream. We turn away from their problems, believing that they are the victims of their own or their parents' irresponsibility, rather than the victims of inexorable social and economic forces. We allow them to be dragged into the vicious cycle of persistent poverty, the "downward spiral, in which the cumulative suction exhausts even heroic effort." Persistent poverty in today's world creates complex needs that can't be met by a single act of assistance.

He emphasizes the high stakes—the deprived and tortured children growing up to fill the nation's prisons, unable to form lasting attachments, to hold decent jobs, and to manage their lives. By contrast, the individuals who move out of poverty consistently have support systems, ranging from a church, labor union, or club to a group of friends who hang out together. These, of course, are the informal support structures—from foster care to police protection—that the formal systems we have relied on have been unable to enlist in achieving common purposes.

Taylor attributes this failure to our insistence on seeing our service systems as a rescue strategy and our inability to see social services as a way of building individual and community capacity. Because he has come to believe that what is now needed are not more interesting projects, but better systems, he considers the issue of scale as critical, and calls for bridging the world of formal public child welfare and the world of the heretofore invisible, informal, extended family and neighborhood supports. He envisages a neighborhood strategy allowing for experimentation with decategorized, comprehensive services that could provide flexible, pro-active responses to a continuum of needs. His experience leads him to the forefront of reformist thinking with respect to social services in general, and child welfare in particular.

Reform in a tragically overwhelmed child welfare system must begin with the recognition that agency-based services alone can never protect children, especially in depleted neighborhoods. Formal services can only supplement the protection and nurturance provided by families and communities. In response to a widespread sense that prevailing child welfare arrangements are too far removed—physically, psychologically, and administratively—from the communities they serve, child welfare agencies throughout the nation are increasingly being asked to establish partnerships with the ultimate child welfare system—families and neighborhoods. The new partnerships anchor help for troubled families in the neighborhoods, by strengthening both formal and informal supports. They involve churches, neighborhood groups, and social workers that come from the same zip code so that families in trouble can be spotted early and provided help, and children can be protected from harm.

The new partnerships emerging between child welfare agencies and communities in many parts of the country involve significant departures from traditional policies and practices. They are bringing mainstream funding to nonprofit community-based agencies that have an entirely different connection with families and neighborhoods than do the agencies that have provided services in the past. Increasingly, the partnerships engage not only community-based organizations, but also parents and neighborhood residents. This allows them to help families feel less isolated in their child-rearing and to respond to a family's self-defined need for help. Partnerships increase the chances that neighbors will help neighbors, be it with a casserole, a port-a-crib, or a baby-sitter. At the same time, strong partnerships in the name of child safety among public and private agencies and parents and neighborhood residents can help to bridge the gulf of mistrust between public agencies and the community. They encourage agencies to measure their effectiveness not on the basis of units of services delivered, but on outcomes achieved for children and families. Taylor joins other child welfare experts in the belief that large-scale human service bureaucracies may actually *be* obsolete, and rather than being refashioned, should be disassembled and replaced by more decentralized, flexible and smaller-scale entities. Because the kind of standardized services that large agencies are used to dispensing no longer meet the need, these new network service organizations may be one early form of replacement.

Taylor calls for youth programs in which caring adults would engage young people in experiences that allow them to imagine a different life story, one that would bring in "the fresh air of possibility and the energy of vision" to support them in living out their alternative stories.

The children who continually witness family and neighborhood violence need to be protected by adults willing to make a commitment to them as mentor, supporter, and model throughout their childhood, because so many of the children from minority cultures are dependent on teachers or other friendly adults to bridge their isolation. Taylor's stories both validate and add to the evidence that "genuine caring and respect" from helping professionals or volunteers are essential to personal transformation.

Taylor has no illusions about the immensity of the challenge. He underscores his "deep commitment to the American vision of an inclusive society where children born in circumstances of poverty have a fair shot at becoming confident, competent adults who are able to support themselves and contribute to the common good." But he also acknowledges that he is writing in an effort to gain the upper hand in his struggle with despair.

Washington Post columnist William Raspberry has written that you don't have to be mean-spirited to turn your back on social problems—you just have to believe that nothing can be done to solve them. In this time of cynicism and of doubt about the value of social action, Fred Taylor's evidence-based plea to citizens to join in protecting children and reforming systems could not be more timely.

The Lazarus Story

Deeply moved once more, Jesus went to the tomb, which was a cave with a stone placed at the entrance. "Take the stone away!" Jesus ordered.

Martha, the dead man's sister, answered, "There will be a bad smell, Lord. He has been buried four days!"

Jesus said to her, "Didn't I tell you that you would see God's glory if you believed?" They took the stone away. Jesus looked up and said, "Thank you, Father, that you listen to me, but I say this for the sake of the people here, so that they will believe that you sent me." After he had said this, he called out in a loud voice, "Lazarus, come out!" He came out, his hands and feet wrapped in grave cloths, and with a cloth around his face. "Untie him," Jesus told them, "and let him go."

John 11:38-44, *Good News Bible*, Today's English Version

Introduction

This book is about a new way of thinking. I'm writing because I am troubled by increasing poverty in a rich land. It troubles me to be confronted on the street by people begging for food, to see homeless men sleeping on grates and old women sitting on park benches with all their earthly goods in shopping bags beside them. It troubles me to see middle class families barely able to make ends meet with both parents working and some working two jobs. I am troubled most of all by children hidden from public view, growing up with no realistic possibility of a decent life.

Fixating on blame and short term solutions to our mounting social problems is not working. The problems are getting worse, and disillusionment increasing to the point of widespread numbness. The alternative is to get clear on what we want and let our planning and implementation be driven by the possibilities of the future rather than the assumptions of the past. The future is empty, still unshaped, unless we fill it with the past. The role of leadership is to create a new and compelling vision capable of steering those who share it to a new place, to develop commitment to the new vision, and to institutionalize the vision. At first the leader may be required to stand in that future in the face of no agreement and speak and live it until others begin to share it.

Politicians on the left and the right speak of taking a "new look at poverty," and developing a "pro-family" public policy. Regrettably, the political debate is deeply polarized. Both major parties cling to divergent antiquated assumptions, and thus speak past each other and a large portion of the American people. Liberals blame poverty on objective conditions in society that they deem correctible by government action. Conservatives blame poverty on subjective conditions within individuals that they deem correctible by the recovery of traditional values. Both are partially right, but their polarization distorts the issues instead of bringing them into clearer focus. In the meantime the center collapses, the plight of the poor worsens, and the stress for families in all classes increases.

Truly, we need more low and moderate income housing, but what do we gain if we pour billions of dollars into housing that is then trashed by tenants who adamantly resist adopting responsible middle-class behaviors? Yes, we want to reduce dependence on alcohol and other drugs and teenage pregnancies, but what is compelling about saying "no" to drugs and sex if they are the only available form of recreation and escape from monotony, and there is no future worth the delay of immediate gratification?

The starting point for a new way of thinking is to give up the fantasy that there was once a golden age to which we can return. What might have been a golden age for one segment of society was a time of torture for other segments—whether it was the antebellum South and slavery, the beginning of the industrial age and child labor, or the multiplication of millionaires in the 1980s and 90s and the simultaneous reappearance of widespread homelessness and hunger.

The poverty and family stress we see today reflect fundamental changes that cannot be reversed. History moves through cycles of breakdown to form new patterns: different ways of governing, doing business, and living in families. What is most troubling about the current liberal-conservative debate is the absence of any clear sense of what we want for the future. Political polarization by ideology guarantees that betterment for one segment of society will be at the expense of another. The sudden collapse of communism should warn us that unenlightened and mendacious capitalism is vulnerable to the same repudiation. Thus, the time is ripe for an evolutionary leap beyond the existing political debate and its narrow, antiquated assumptions to a broader, deeper conversation with assumptions that enable us to progress in an interdependent, global society.

This book offers a perspective that engages both the objective and subjective conditions that play out in poverty or prosperity. It is about rethinking poverty. It is about new paradigms that move beyond either—

or to holistic strategies, paradigms that evoke fresh energy and lead to inclusive outcomes. While not a new way of thinking historically, it is different from the thinking that currently shapes political debate and media reporting.

The current political polarization is contributing to the formation of a permanent underclass. Reestablishing a political center that aligns the energies of all classes for positive action will not be easy. Moreover, the consequences of past neglect will be with us for a long time. Political promises of a "quick fix" are obscene. There is no quick fix for the thousands of people whose brains did not grow to their full capacity as babies because they did not get enough food or the right kind of food or never bonded with a parent figure. However, it is possible to stop these destructive patterns from repeating. We cannot prevent the damage that has already occurred, but in many cases we can heal some of it and reduce the production of further damage.

When severely deprived and abused children grow up, they have difficulty forming lasting attachments, holding jobs, and managing their lives. Our prisons are full of such individuals. Unless we find the way to both prevent and heal psychological, spiritual, and economic disabling of children, the demand for more and more prisons and institutions for unwanted children—and the taxes to finance them—will only increase. The easy access to cheap addictive drugs and guns exacerbates the danger for all of us, especially the children trapped in poverty.

In 1968, the Kerner Commission, charged with investigating the urban riots of that time, warned that this country was splitting into two Americas—one given access to the opportunities that lead to prosperity, and the other left behind in unchanging poverty. Another generation has come of age since that report was published, and the situation is worse.

We have always had poverty in this country. Most Americans are descended from immigrants who arrived in this "land of opportunity" with the clothes on their backs and little else. But somehow these hearty souls made a place for themselves and gave the next generation a better place to start. The American experiment worked for these people.

For two groups in American culture—African Americans and Native Americans—the situation was very different. African Americans had to face two centuries under the horror of human slavery and another century of legalized segregation. Native Americans were driven from their land and segregated in reservations, entirely cut off from the opportunities available to the 18th- and 19th-century immigrants from Europe and today's Asian immigrants.

The Civil Rights Movement of the 1960s succeeded in dismantling forced segregation, although racism itself continued only slightly abated. Large numbers of educated and prepared African Americans and some Native Americans rapidly entered the social mainstream, but those not educationally or psychologically prepared ran into a new set of problems.

At the time legal segregation was dismantled, the American economy was undergoing radical change. Familiar, accessible jobs in farming, heavy industry, and the trades were disappearing. Emerging jobs that paid a living wage required sophisticated skills and above-average education. Unprepared African Americans and Native Americans were simply left behind. And we began to notice that those left behind were not all people of color. The majority of poor in this country are white. Many great grandchildren of European immigrants slipped backwards into poverty. Liberal politicians tried to create a kind of "safety net" to protect those left behind, particularly the children, from a sub-human existence. The proposed solution was expanding government entitlement programs, but these were only stopgap measures. These programs did not support movement into the mainstream for millions of children, women, and men. It is these persons and their offspring who are not participating in the great American experiment today.

We don't have to accept this—not the homelessness, not the deprivation and abuse of children, not the unconscionable gap between poor and comfortable, not the development of a permanent social underclass, not the current impotence of both major political parties to engage with the crisis, not the offense to our moral consciousness and religious sensibilities. I'm writing to say that we as private citizens, and public officials, as well as churches, synagogues, public agencies, and community groups can empower ourselves to make a difference, starting in the neighborhood, town, or city where we live.

Throwing ourselves frenetically at human need or simply pouring more money into programs will not make a difference. These approaches guarantee burnout, resentment, and deepening despair. We have to open our hearts first to the deep apathy in this country and in ourselves. Under this apathy is the repressed rage of unlived life—in the poor, but also in the comfortable. This rage has to come to consciousness and then be transmuted into passion for constructive change.

And we have to use our heads. We must examine our assumptions, and be willing to let go those that hinder more than help. We must learn to think in new ways about issues that touch us deeply. We need to get beyond outrage at poverty, child neglect, and violence to think clearly and exert the initiative and teamwork it takes to make a difference.

In the early 1960s, a friend introduced me to the idea of "social energy," the gathering of commitment and action around a common vision of a new arrangement in society. I felt this energy as I participated in the 1963 March on Washington and listened spellbound as Martin Luther King, Jr. gave his "I have a dream" speech. Something happened in me that day, as it did in many others—an inner shift from suppressed anger about conditions in this country to an enlivened sense of possibility, and a wish to translate my values and aspirations into action.

I was then pastor of a suburban Baptist church, married with three small children—and restless. A traditional vocational trail had led me from a religious family in Princeton, Kentucky, to college at Vanderbilt University. There I experienced a call to the ministry, so I went to Yale Divinity School and then earned another degree in Biblical studies from Southern Baptist Theological Seminary in Louisville, Kentucky. I was all set to spend my life as a local church pastor when this idea of creative "social energy" began to gnaw at me.

A *Washington Post* editorial about a church near
the U.S. Capitol selling its building and moving to the
suburbs caught my eye. The editorial said, in effect,
"good decision," for the church had shown no interest
in the surrounding community, and the community
deemed it a sign of progress for that congregation to
move on and let someone else have the real estate. I
had previously asked that church to hold a graduation
ceremony for a nearby job training center in their
sanctuary. The reply was, "No, we don't want to
desecrate the sanctuary." What did they mean? That
black people were not welcome? Or that a secular
activity like honoring job training graduates would
diminish the "spirituality" of their space?

Listening to King at the Lincoln Memorial and
reading that editorial connected with my friend's
observations about "social energy." And that
connection helped me discern my own call as a
minister. It also touched on a very important
theological question. How did my view of a personal
God relate to forming and releasing social energy to
realize our highest and deepest social ideals? I felt I
was being led toward a ministry that would somehow
answer this question.

Several years before, I had met Reverend Gordon
Cosby, the minister of the ecumenical Church of the
Saviour in downtown Washington, DC. As a first-year
divinity student, I had heard Gordon Cosby present a vision
of the local church cultivating a community of love and
support among its own members, and moving out from
this base to create structures that empower those who have
lost heart. I wanted to be part of this kind of church.

With my young family in tow, I resigned my pastorate and looked for a secular job in order to be involved with the Church of the Saviour. We arrived at an opportune time. Gordon had recently participated in civil rights demonstrations in Selma, Alabama. He was moved deeply by the spiritual vitality he had seen in the African American family with whom he stayed. He sensed a powerful stirring of the Spirit among the black churches of Selma. When he returned, he asked himself how he might make a difference to the poor in Washington, DC.

One day he read a story in *The Washington Post* about a local children's institution, Junior Village. At a time when most cities had phased out institutional care for children, the nation's capital had allowed a temporary shelter for abandoned, abused, and neglected children to grow from an average daily population of 200 in 1962 to 912 in 1965. It was the largest children's institution in the country. Gordon believed that children belong in homes, not institutions, and that the city could change the situation if it was challenged. He preached a series of sermons that advocated replacing Junior Village with community-based alternatives. Out of his preaching, an organization, For Love of Children (FLOC), was born. I became involved as a volunteer at the beginning, and a year later was employed as FLOC's first full-time director. In this book, I am mining FLOC's 30 plus years of experience and my own study for what they offer to the struggle to realize generative conditions that support development toward prosperity for all Americans.

AN OVERVIEW

I have organized this book around the central metaphor of a Biblical story—the raising of Lazarus from the dead in John 11:38-44. The book is divided into three parts. In Part One, "The Crisis of Increasing Child Poverty, Abuse, Neglect," I draw the analogy between the state of Lazarus in the tomb and the situation of persistently poor children and families today, and between the resignation of Lazarus' family and neighbors to his death and the resignation of this country to a permanent underclass. Part Two, "Action: A Small Church Takes On a City Government," tells the remarkable story of a small church-spawned organization, For Love of Children, taking on the District of Columbia government to open the "tomb" of Junior Village, a deprivative government-run warehouse for abandoned, abused, and neglected children. Part Three, "Reflection: Rethinking Old Assumptions," challenges traditional liberal and conservative paradigms of thinking about poverty and social change with emerging new paradigms for social analysis and action.

This book is written for both religious and secular audiences. My aspiration is to broaden and deepen the conversation for justice for children and families and draw in other stakeholders besides already active child and family advocates and service providers. I aim to speak to the mother moving from welfare to work as well as to her social worker, to clergy and laity looking for ways to stand for social justice in their local communities, and to both politicians and citizens who are seeking fresh ways to language their concerns and proposals.

I have attempted particularly to address two audiences who often speak past each other. One is the religious community who resonate to the intuitive and evocative language of metaphor and story. The other is the secular community who resonate more naturally to empirical data and analysis. We need each other to achieve a just society. I hope my use of metaphor, story, social analysis, and paradigm analysis will contribute to the emergence of a common, compelling vision that calls us into creative action that will powerfully benefit society's most vulnerable children and families.

Part One

THE CRISIS OF INCREASING
CHILD POVERTY, ABUSE, NEGLECT

Chapter One

LAZARUS IN THE TOMB AS
METAPHOR FOR THE CRISIS

I want to tell you the story of a dead man and how he came alive again. I see this story as a powerful metaphor for understanding the complex nature of poverty and envisioning a future free of its shackles.

The story of Lazarus shows powerlessness in the extreme. To all human appearances, Lazarus is dead—dead and entombed. His body is decaying. He has been written off. Nothing more can be expected from Lazarus. His life is finished. Yet Jesus says, "If you believe, you'll see the glory of God, God at work. You'll see things you never thought were possible."

Jesus is an agent of a higher power, but he doesn't do this raising from the dead as some kind of dramatic solo. He involves the community of friends, family, and onlookers in his work. He involves them with Lazarus, the one written off as dead, the one who has apparently passed out of the realm of human usefulness or possibility. He calls forth their power to help free Lazarus to claim his own power.

POWER IN ACTION:
ROLL AWAY THE STONE

Having followed Jesus to the site, the friends and family of Lazarus stand around the tomb wondering, "What on earth does this healer have in mind?" They are intrigued, puzzled, a little frightened. Then Jesus speaks. He gives the community an assignment: "Roll away the stone."

This makes no sense. Everybody knows that when you're dead, that's it. Nothing's left—no power, no energy, no life. Moreover, after three days, a dead man is going to smell. It would be better not to let the stench out. Why be exposed to that? Let's just keep it covered up.

Jesus repeats his command. The people are astonished, but finally they go along with him. Gathering their collective strength, and against their better judgment, they roll away the stone. Then they stand back.

RECIPROCAL POWER:
LAZARUS, COME FORTH

To their amazement, Jesus starts calling into the abyss of the tomb. He shouts loudly, as if someone is asleep in there. He calls the dead person by name, "Lazarus, come forth!"

Lo and behold, the lifeless one hears. The dead one responds. He from whom nothing further can be expected comprehends. He hears his name and comes forth. The calling of his name empowers Lazarus, and he uses that power to grope toward the light, the fresh air, the new possibilities. He stands at the cave opening, blinking in the harsh light of day. His friends gasp and step further back, dumbstruck. Lazarus is there, alive. But he is still enshrouded. The grave cloths are still wrapped around his arms and legs. He is still constrained, still bound.

SHARING POWER: UNBIND HIM

Then comes the final command. Jesus tells the community to stay with the job they've begun. They must unbind and liberate Lazarus from the grave wrappings, the powerlessness of death, so he can move freely in the world.

When they unwrap him, Lazarus opens his arms to his friends. He is alive again. He begins to experience ordinary human events. When we next read about him, he is entertaining Jesus at supper.

The story of Jesus and the community raising Lazarus from the dead is a story of power empowering powerlessness and action transforming resignation. Jesus has the vision of God about to do something. He aligns himself with that vision. He stands in a future of possibility for Lazarus and the community, and generates action. He calls upon the community, who have resigned themselves to Lazarus' demise, to help him, to roll away the stone and then to unbind the now living man.

But the resurrection of Lazarus is not just up to Jesus, the community, and the higher power. The situation requires that Lazarus hear his name being called and mobilize himself to come forth. This story is a parable of reciprocal power, of active power used to evoke latent power—the power of the surrounding community and the power of the powerless.

TRANSLATING THE STORY

What does this story have to say about entrenched poverty and vulnerable children and other left-behind persons in one of the richest nations on earth?

In a country where most find gratifying opportunity, and a few achieve enormous prosperity, a remnant of Americans live in degradation and hopelessness. Our national myth says that anyone, no matter how humble in origin, can make it in America. For many, this is undeniably the case. But for a significant remnant it is not.

About 10 percent of the population is left behind at the bottom of society, like a dead Lazarus, unlikely to rise. The majority of this remnant are women and children, but there are also large numbers of men—many in prison, and many who no longer figure in the unemployment statistics because they have given up looking for work. These children, women, and men exist outside the mainstream and are likely to stay outside until a deliberate process is initiated to include them as full participants.

I am suggesting a new conversation that upsets commonly held ideas and assumptions. This conversation requires inventing both language and systems that support the poor in thriving.

WHO ARE THE POOR?

Who are these poor people who appear to be permanently living at the bottom of American society? Research shows that in the relatively prosperous decade from 1970 to 1980, one quarter of the U.S. population fell below the poverty line for at least one year. For most of these individuals and families, their stay in poverty was temporary, induced by divorce, illness, or job loss. By getting well, getting a new job, or remarrying, they moved out of poverty with little dependence on government programs.[1]

A much smaller percentage stayed in poverty for at least eight out of the ten years of the study. Researchers identified them as the "persistently poor," who remain in poverty year after year, as distinct from the "temporarily poor," for whom poverty, although exceedingly traumatic, is time limited.[2]

The persistently poor, of whom the large majority are women and children, are currently positioned to be a permanent part of our social system. By the standards of basic human decency, and by any religious standards, in this affluent country, it is unacceptable that women, men, and especially children be hungry, ill housed, or in desperate poverty. In making this statement, however, I do not imply that we simply need more of the same social programs that have already been justified with similar moral assertions. We need to follow a different paradigm, one that supports the poor in thriving both economically and spiritually.

WHERE DO WE START?

We first need to look beyond our stereotypes of the persistently poor to see the real people. We need to overcome our knee-jerk reactions—recoiling and distancing ourselves from them, and then designing sterile institutions and interventions that "save" poor people at little personal risk to the rest of us. We must walk together into the territory of the persistently poor, who, only slightly better off than Lazarus, are barely alive in the tomb. We cannot write them off as the invisible, rotting flesh of humanity from whom nothing is expected. We must see them and hear them. Only then will we grasp what is needed for them and ourselves to become free, self-determining, contributing participants in a new society.

WHO ARE THE PERSISTENTLY POOR?

Picture a 30-year-old mother who never had a childhood, who was pressed into the role of parent at age six or eight or ten by her mother or father. Now she is trapped on public assistance, hating her dependency, but afraid to risk going back to school or job training because she doesn't have day care, or because the known seems safer than the unknown. Her release from the incredible monotony of her existence is to use a $5 rock of crack cocaine and pay for it by selling her body on the street, or give herself to "her man," who is in and out of the house as he chooses, and sometimes leaves behind some money.

Picture a six-month-old child whose only stimulation is the swinging light bulb over the crib. The persistently poor are the thousands of children who are literally raising themselves, or whose care is taken over by a slightly older child—maybe a six-year-old as principal caregiver to a two-year-old. These are true examples.

The face of the persistently poor is the 25-year-old male who never saw a role model going off to work every day and bringing home a regular paycheck. He gets his picture of being a man from men hanging out on the streets, or from the fantasy land of television, and he can't understand why the outside world doesn't tolerate his coming to work when he feels like it.

It's the face of an eight-year-old first grader whose diet is so inadequate that he can't sit still or concentrate for more than 30 seconds at a time.

It's the face of an abandoned, neglected child in foster care, whose psychological problems are ignored by the child welfare system. Some children bounce from foster home to foster home until they reach adolescence and, in too many cases, bounce into the juvenile correction system. Some start life abandoned at birth in the hospital. For them the system sometimes provides a clean, well-run institution with caregivers changing every eight hours, supplemented by smiling, cooing volunteers. But even at its best, good physical care is not enough. A child's most crucial need is lifelong bonding with a parent figure who is also bonded with the child, and inclusion in a family that gives social and legal status.

By the standards of the larger society, the persistently poor, including children and adults who were seriously deprived as children, tend to be emotionally, physically, and educationally underdeveloped. Their incompetence, passive aggressiveness, and "attention deficits" are predictable.

The persistently poor are also independent-minded, hard-working parents holding down two and three jobs to feed, clothe, and shelter their children. They remain in low-paying jobs in areas where housing costs are out of reach for low-income people. Some families have lost their foothold in the middle class and survive by sharing an apartment with another family, until tensions erupt and one family ends up on the streets. These families may cycle in and out of emergency shelters at a cost to the taxpayer of $500 and up per week. They get free meals, and even maid service, but little serious support for regaining their independence. They are served by a system consumed with putting out fires in a way that generally destroys what it tries to save. By "taking care" of the homeless in ways that shift to the government the burden for such basic responsibilities as paying rent and buying and cooking food, we destroy initiative and create dependence and apathy.

In brief, the persistently poor are those largely anonymous women, men, and children who have retreated into or never emerged from what Brazilian educator Paulo Freire calls the "culture of silence." There is a profound miscommunication between them and the larger society, which the poor experience as inferiority. Seeing themselves as inferior limits the options available to them.

Unable to make themselves heard, they settle for the leftovers in housing, medical care, jobs, and education. Unable to communicate the potentially creative power of their rage and longing, they settle for the subsistence government and community programs hand out. And they are expected to be grateful. Conservatives say these people remain within boundaries of their own making—lack of initiative and discipline. Liberals see the trap as external, and blame it on government inaction.

THE CRITICAL ISSUE: POWERLESSNESS

In a way we are just beginning to understand, the powerlessness of one segment of society undermines the powerfulness of the rest. We used to think that the persistently poor were irrelevant to the future of this country. The mainstream could delegate the moral task of helping the poor and the political task of containing social unrest to government programs and "do-gooder" private charities. But entrenched, intergenerational poverty is showing us that containment doesn't work. Poor youths, from whom mainstream society expects nothing, do not go away. Many join the enemy, and participate in the undermining of society through drug trafficking and violence. Babies who receive no prenatal care do not disappear, but enter society with lifelong mental and physical defects. Some need to be maintained all their lives at great public and private expense.

Power is the ability to influence others, to engage in exchange, and to cause an outcome. Powerlessness is dependence upon outside forces to make good things happen. Persistent poverty breeds powerlessness as social condition and state of mind. The ability to exchange, to cause events and outcomes, empowers. We need to think seriously about empowering rather than containing the poor. But first we need to understand the conditions under which the poor are living, because these conditions generate a sense of powerlessness.

The editorial writer Michael Barone said, "We are a nation of rich adults and poor children. Pay heed to [Daniel Patrick] Moynihan's words, 'The future of a society may be forecast by how it cares for its young.' ... A society of rich adults and poor children can become a society of poor adults, poor children, and poor old people."[3] Barone adds that since the problem of poverty activates no constituencies with any clout, the impetus for change must come from logic. I submit it will take logic as well as a constituency who understand the organic relationship between the plight of the poor and the health of the whole country. South African Bishop Desmond Tutu reminds us of the Zulu proverb that when the foot picks up a thorn the whole body must stop and attend to it.

A PERSONAL NOTE

I often use the Lazarus story to think about our mission and purpose at For Love of Children. Some nonprofit organizations focus entirely on public policy. Others concentrate on providing direct services. FLOC has attempted to do both. FLOC's initial goal was to roll away the stone of public policy and community inertia that perpetuated a 900-bed, 19th-century public institution called Junior Village for homeless, abused, and neglected children from six months to eighteen years of age. I relate this experience in Chapters Five and Six to show how focused community action can carry out the directive "Roll away the stone."

In the course of that struggle we developed both direct service and advocacy programs. Between 1972 and 1984, FLOC operated an attorney-led Child Advocacy Center to tackle the legislative, budgetary, and policy issues that affect homeless, abused, and neglected children and their families in the District of Columbia. The FLOC Child Advocacy Center floundered in 1984. We were broke and Center staff were burned out. However, we gradually expanded our direct service programs and from that base continued to advocate for system change.

FLOC now operates a foster home program for 120 children, a therapeutic group home for 10 adolescent boys, a psycho-educational alternative school for 50 adolescents with special learning and emotional needs, a transitional housing and counseling program for families in need of assistance, an educational advocacy program for children with special needs, an outdoor adventure challenge and camping program that enables youths and parents to transcend their self-imposed limits, a home visitation and parent coaching program for 75 poor, overburdened, first time mothers and babies; foster care, group home, and independent living and training for 15 teen moms and babies; and a neighborhood after school and evening tutoring program for 250 elementary and junior high children.

In succeeding chapters I will draw upon my FLOC experience to explore different facets of the Lazarus story. Biblical scholar Walter Brueggemann reminds us that the Bible uses language to push toward new possibilities. It uses the language of story and metaphor not so much to define as to evoke. This language is very different than the language of company memoranda or official reports. It is full of ambiguity and profoundly creative. Much of the Bible is poetic. Its images burrow beneath our defenses and self-satisfaction, then confront us from within ourselves.

Metaphors are powerful mind changers. They are created when diverse images are placed side by side for our contemplation—for example, the barely alive poor and the dead Lazarus. To make sense of the connection, the reader must mentally leap back and forth, and be drawn beyond customary ways of thinking. Mental boundaries are breached, and images of new possibilities surface. Metaphor has the creative power to evoke and shape the energy of an individual, a group, even a nation.

To conceive real social transformation requires rearranging our mental furniture. Some time-honored political, social, and religious assumptions will have to go. This process of change will involve both the heart and the mind, both the intuitive grasp of fresh possibilities and the practical discernment to move toward them step by step. The process must align people of good will from diverse religious, political, and social traditions who work together to realize a compelling vision. The vision of the local communities and this nation supporting the inclusion of all citizens in our collective abundance will burst old boundaries of thinking, such as the traditional meeting-basic-needs strategy of liberals or the return of traditional values prescribed by conservatives.

Joseph Campbell said that what most people yearn for is to experience themselves as truly alive. The vision I see will mean a major shift in priorities for the already comfortable—from accumulation of possessions for security to enrichment of experience, the experience of being truly alive. This shift, in turn, could lead to a whole new economy—an experience-oriented economy that would present far better possibilities to the poor than the current consumption-based economy. But this is getting ahead of the Lazarus story, which starts with the bleak reality of a dead man walled off by a huge stone rolled over the entrance of his tomb.

Chapter Two

THE PAIN OF POVERTY

The persistently poor are in the same boat as persons with AIDS, the physically deformed, the chronically ill, and the dying of all ages. Their condition is intimidating to those who are well and in comfortable circumstances. Out of sight, out of mind is the typical response. But like people with AIDS, the persistently poor are becoming too numerous and too visible to ignore. And more is at stake than the value of being comfortable. Friends of persons dying with AIDS testify to the powerful humanizing experience of being there with and for their friend, who may initially have been a stranger.

The Lazarus story is about transformation inside and outside the tomb. Jesus leads the community into proximity to the dead man, so they cannot help but get emotionally involved. They are in a position to see, hear, and, most poignantly, smell the situation. They must be there and do as they are told, regardless of what they are feeling.

Doctors, nurses, and other helping professionals go through a cathartic process in their training and practice which enables them to feel and then put aside their emotions of fear and avoidance in order to give their full attention to the person before them.

To grapple with human suffering in any form, from child abuse to hunger and homelessness, requires an uncommon attentiveness which is characteristic of that level of human generosity we call love. Love is essentially the exercise of freedom to take in another's presence, invite their speaking, and speak out of our listening.

One can be in solidarity with the poor without being poor, just as the well can minister to the sick. Everyone has to carry their own burden. This applies to the one in five American children who are growing up in grinding poverty as well as to the four in five who are better off. The point is to move close enough to take in what is going on and notice the possibilities of making the burden manageable or even lifting it off.

A LEAP OF IMAGINATION

The story of Lazarus can help us understand our predicament and our possibility as citizens of a rich country with an outrageous remnant of poverty. The journey requires imagination. We must experience, at least imaginatively, the conditions the persistently poor are facing to get past our instinctive emotional reactions. Then we can imagine a community that works for everyone, that awakens these same children and adults to their potential to take charge of their lives and supports them in their self-development.

A Buddhist meditation provides an exercise for getting past instinctive emotional reactions to a place of compassionate objectivity. The meditation involves vividly imagining our own corpse as it passses through stages from coldness to decomposition, then to bare skeleton, finally to dust. The use of this meditation, ironically enough, is said to bring a sense of peace and joy. This is the idea—that we need a leap of imagination to mentally engage conditions of extreme poverty until we get beyond our normal repulsion.

ACKNOWLEDGING POVERTY AS IT IS

Can you imagine what it is like to be desperately poor all your life? Can you imagine living year after year in rundown, unsafe, unsanitary living conditions, wearing dirty, ill-fitting clothes? Imagine what it is like to live in cramped spaces with no privacy and no place to read or study. Imagine your children playing in the alley with scraps of wood and metal or discarded syringes for toys. What is it like to never have enough money? Or education? Or job skills? To have access only to indifferent crisis health care?

Can you imagine being the caretaker for three of your own children and two of your 15-year-old daughter's children? Or imagine being a four-year-old child in an institution, having no parent to count on, no siblings you know? Imagine what it would feel like to watch TV and see people there who have everything they want; and to see no one on that screen who has a life like yours.

How does it feel to be written about as a social problem, described as a drain on the national budget? What is it like to be invisible because people choose not to look at you or acknowledge you in any way? What is it like to know that no one expects anything of you, that your possibilities are few, that your life will always be like this?

Imagine receiving no acknowledgment of your specialness, even of the small ways in which you are gifted. Imagine having to keep all your dreams to yourself, lest they be put down. What is it like to see no way out, no hope?

IDENTIFYING WITH THE POWERLESS

Such imagining can transform your mind. So also can real life experiences. I caught a glimpse of this transformation process a few years ago on an Outward Bound course. Outward Bound is an international program that challenges the physical, emotional, and spiritual limits we put on ourselves.

I spent 26 days hiking, white water canoeing, sailing, and rowing in the ocean off the coast of Maine, rock climbing, doing a ropes course, spending three days alone with minimal food, and doing a two-day service project. We were seven men and five women, living in the out-of-doors the entire time.

One day we took several handicapped children from a state assessment center on an overnight camping trip. My partner Charlie and I were assigned to 10-year-old Frankie. He was blind, too paralyzed to walk or to move his arms except with a jerky motion, and unable to speak except for a few repetitive words.

Charlie and I fed Frankie by hand, changed his diaper, and pushed him in his wheelchair into the lake to feel the water. Frankie squealed with delight. At night we sat around a campfire, singing songs and telling stories. He couldn't sing, but he sat enthralled by the activity, and comforted by the touch of bodies on all sides of him.

To enter his very complicated world of survival operations, I had to slow my life down to Frankie's pace. I connected with buried parts of myself: remembering what a privilege it is to chew food, being humbled by simple tactile experiences—water, the breeze, the annoyance of mosquitos. Most of the time I zoom past these sensations, but with Frankie, I had to stop in my tracks. I was in a position of power. I could cause events to happen. Frankie could not. Between us was the incredible gap between the powerful and the powerless. But in our encounter, difference met difference, and we were both awakened.

Jesus said that it's harder for a camel to go through the eye of a needle than for a rich man to enter the kingdom of God. Maybe being totally present to my silent friend Frankie was the eye of the needle. My natural inclination is to avoid people like him, to spend my time being busy and productive. But with Frankie, I was able to enter totally into the present moment with all its richness. It was like seeing the wonder of life under a huge microscope, when I'm used to observing life on the run. Frankie was powerless, and I'm deathly afraid of powerlessness. Most of us crave at least a critical minimum of power—to be in control of our own lives. To relate to powerless people thrusts us into uncharted situations. We crave doing. But all we really need is being, to be with the person and be centered in ourselves. That's what they want from us—to allow ourselves as we are to be with them as they are. This lesson, I have learned from other Frankies, leads to joy.

JUNIOR VILLAGE

The euphemistic name Junior Village glossed over the tomb-like qualities of a huge public institution for 900 homeless children in Washington, DC. It was located on a 20-acre reservation overlooking the Potomac River that had formerly been used as a training school for delinquent boys.

The children were divided according to age and sex, which meant breaking up siblings. Adolescents were housed in turn-of-the-century dormitories. Each room contained a row of 20 or so bunk beds and foot lockers. Small children were placed in cottages designed for 30 to 40 children each—one for crib babies, another for toddlers, another for four- and five-year-olds. The institution was often so crowded that babies slept two to a bed.

School-age children traveled to public schools in orange buses with the lettering Junior Village. In their schools they were identified by the bus that brought them—as "Junior Village children."

Children, from six months of age to 18, were placed in Junior Village as an emergency arrangement to allow social workers time to resolve family problems or to line up a foster home. The average length of stay was six months. Some children stayed for years.

When I visited the toddler cottage in 1966, with 10 other adults, 20 two- and three-year-olds pushed and shoved for position, begging to be picked up. I lifted an African American child who patted my white face and asked, "Are you my mommy?" I looked into her searching eyes, swallowed, and said, "No, honey, I'm not your mommy." My reply made no difference. She squeezed me around the neck, pressing her head tightly against mine. When I tried to set her down, she clung even more tightly. I turned to a woman attendant for help.

A few months later I took a group of FLOC volunteers on a tour of the institution. A grandmother who had served for years on a small-town hospital board was impressed with the freshly painted walls, clean waxed floors, and white-uniformed attendants. At the end of the tour she asked, "Fred, why are you so troubled by this facility? Everything seems quite in order to me." A few yards away a five-year-old boy asked, "Daddy, why are these children in jail?"

Junior Village was not a jail, nor a place where children were intentionally mistreated, although physical and sexual abuse did happen. In some cases incidents of abuse were reported and the administration did nothing. In other cases, staff looked the other way as bullies established a pecking order. The beds were soft and the bedding clean. The children were fed wholesome food, bathed, and issued clean clothes each day. Many of the staff were gentle and kind. And yet it was a tomb, lacking the basic ingredients for human nurture and development: a parent or other consistent, caring adult with whom each child could bond, the intimate sibling connections we take for granted in a family, and the right to have personal possessions.

Children at Junior Village were not allowed to own their clothing or toys, for fear of the competition that would follow. A *Harpers* magazine article appearing that year, entitled "A Special Hell for Children in Washington," by J.W. Anderson, described Junior Village as "a factory for mental illness on the banks of the Potomac." A large, all-purpose, catch-all institution is incontrovertibly a tomb for children deprived of deep emotional nurturing in a bonded relationship with a parent. The three-year-old who had forgotten what her mother looked like and the five-year-old visitor who thought he was in a jail knew better than any adult that Junior Village was like Lazarus' tomb.

MILDRED JONES

In the early days of FLOC, one of our volunteers heard about a young African American woman with five children living illegally in the janitor's quarters of an apartment building. The volunteer, Jessie Ashton, an African American herself, made a visit to the apartment. The building was one of those huge red brick apartment

SAVING AMERICA'S CHILDREN

buildings, formerly fancy, now seedy: open windows with no screens, woodwork needing paint, dirt instead of landscaping, and the ubiquitous trash piles scattered inside and outside.

When Mildred Jones answered the door, Jessie said, "I'm a neighbor. I hear you're having problems. Can I talk to you?" Mildred silently and cautiously let her in. The children were watching TV. Mildred invited her to sit down and then fell back into silence. Jessie tried to get a conversation going, but Mildred had trouble getting words out.

Jessie had never seen a more frightened person. After a half hour of one-way conversation, Jessie said, "I've got to go now, but I'd like to come back to see you. May I?" Mildred nodded her head yes.

Jessie went back the next day and the next. The same scenario repeated itself. Jessie wondered if there were any point to her visiting, but she was touched by Mildred's situation. Her body was like a zombie's—tight and frozen in place—but in her eyes there was feeling.

Visiting Mildred reminded Jessie of a time of paralysis in her own childhood. At age 12 she had lived with an aunt in a slum apartment. The aunt had to work at night, and Jessie was left alone. She was instructed by her aunt not to open the door for anyone. One night she was awakened by a loud banging on the door and a drunken voice threatening to break the door down. Jessie scampered into the closet and prayed with all her might to be spared. The man went away, but the memory stayed. She decided to visit Mildred again, and to share that painful

CHAPTER TWO 37

memory. Mildred listened intently, still saying nothing, but as Jessie left, Mildred squeezed her hand appreciatively.

On the fourth visit, Mildred finally said a few words; trust was beginning to build. On the succeeding day, Mildred's story came out. She and her five children had been living with her aunt and four other people in a small apartment. She had had two children as a teenager, then married at age 20 and had three more. Her husband left her when they were evicted from their apartment.

At that time, her aunt offered to take her in temporarily if Mildred would share her public assistance. The visit stretched into a year. During this time she became involved with the janitor in another apartment building, who invited Mildred and her children to move in. The apartment went with his job, he said, and her welfare check was enough to buy their food and clothing. Between them they might even have a little bit left over. It looked like a good arrangement.

What they didn't reckon with was the "man in the house" law in the District of Columbia at that time: any woman observed by a welfare inspector to have a continuing relationship with an able-bodied male could have her welfare check terminated immediately. Moreover, the Welfare Department was conducting a campaign to "purge welfare cheaters" from public assistance.

The inspectors worked shifts, the night shift often sitting in cars watching the comings and goings of welfare recipients. Mildred was observed to be in a continuing relationship with an able-bodied man, and her check was dropped. When this happened the janitor left, so when Jessie Ashton knocked on Mildred's door, she found a very dependent woman of 26, so overwhelmed with fear that she could not talk.

She had a ninth-grade education, and her work experience was limited to domestic and dishwashing jobs. She was terrified of losing her children, afraid the next person to come to her door might be a social worker to take them away. For all practical purposes she was entombed.

Approximately two out of three persons in persistent poverty live in families like Mildred's. The women typically have less than a high school education, their schooling interrupted by teenage pregnancies. Many are unable to get and hold a job paying above a poverty wage—this in a society that already penalizes women by paying them 69- 75% the wages of men at the same educational levels. When they do get work, they have to find day care for the children, which eats up much of their income.

Advancing in jobs is difficult. Working overtime would show initiative and thus improve their chances for promotion, but day care facilities have limited hours. Housing costs have skyrocketed to the point that even two-parent families with both parents working cannot support a family on entry-level wages.

Reginald, raised in a FLOC foster home, left at age 18 to be on his own. He did pretty well for a while. But his debts kept piling up and he decided to sell drugs to pay them off. It looked easy, but he got caught and was sent to the penitentiary for a year. When he got out, he decided to avoid that trap. He got a food preparation job at slightly above minimum wage.

Borrowing from friends, he made the necessary deposit to get an efficiency apartment. That lasted until winter, when he received a huge gas bill for heat. With that, he just left the place, and went to live with his sister. She was later evicted.

This was his situation when he came to see me. He wanted to know if FLOC had an apartment to rent. I told him we didn't, but that I'd be glad to help him explore other possibilities. Here was somebody who didn't have to be in a permanent underclass, or end up a dead young man, or in prison. He could climb, but he needed encouragement to find a realistic way out.

He was bright, his vocabulary was impressive, and he could articulate his ideas. Asked about his finances, he said his take home pay was about $500 a month. He really wanted to marry his girlfriend, but didn't want to until he could "take care of her." "You might just have a lot of false pride there," I suggested. "Why not consider a 50-50 partnership?" He shook his head; it didn't seem to him like being a "man."

Reginald could go either way: he could resume selling drugs or he could find a support system to make his way legally in the world. Studies have shown that the individuals who move out of poverty consistently have support systems, which range from a church, labor union, or club to a group of friends who hang out at a particular bar.

Reginald is one of the young black men of whom Americans are reputedly more afraid than any other single group. Because of our fear we have some stake in keeping them entombed. And many of these young black men end up literally dead. A black man in America stands a 1 in 21 chance of being murdered, compared to a 1 in 131 chance for a white man, or a 1 in 369 chance for a white woman. Homicide is the leading cause of death for young black males.

WHY WE DON'T SEE THE POOR

Many screens separate the poor and the comfortable. One is ignorance. Another is fear. People with power generally know very little about those without it, although the poor are quite good at "reading" the comfortable. The comfortable are conditioned to image the poor as dead weight, or worse, as insatiable in their need. The poor are conditioned to see the comfortable as intimidated by poverty, ready to run; therefore they must settle for easy-to-give handouts without serious confrontation. Everyone conspires to keep the lid on the fear and the rage. Occasionally the rage of the poor overflows into urban riots. As soon as order is restored, the rage goes underground.

When I write about entrapped people, I am not saying that the individual human beings who are persistently poor lack worth or that their lives mean less than others. Rather, this is how poor people are thought of: they are not considered contributing members of this culture, with gifts, inclinations, goals, and dreams to bring to the common good. In this sense, they are entombed, and apparently, that is where we want them. Their decomposition is mostly out of range, so the rest of us can go on with our lives. Sometimes we can't see them because we feel overwhelmed. Our social problems are so big and so complicated that there seems nothing we can do. If experts—sociologists, psychologists, economists, state and federal officials—can't solve the problem, how can ordinary individuals hope to deal with it? This is the most crippling assumption of all—that someone else knows about it and can fix it, but I can't.

If we open our eyes we can see as clearly as the experts what some of the problems are, and can figure out ways to make a difference. Sometimes we can't see because we believe poor people are willfully ignorant, or are lazy and unmotivated. They could escape if they wanted to. We turn away because we believe the poor are the victims of their own or their parent's irresponsibility, caught in the consequences of human error. There is very little that anyone can do to reverse the consequences.

This kind of refusal to see the poor robs us all of our simple humanity and our interconnectedness. It renders us impotent to do justice in the face of a complex set of social neglects.

POVERTY: A DOWNWARD SPIRAL

The complexity of poverty is a downward spiral, the erosion of energy, vision, and resources. Seen this way, poverty is not just a problem for poor individuals. It is a collective problem of neighborhoods, cities, states, nations, the whole planet. It affects us collectively, as a system. Just as a downwardly spiraling marriage cannot be separated into what is his problem and what is hers, so poverty is a dynamic dysfunctioning that affects the poor and the institutions, systems, policies, and individuals who make up the whole society. Poverty challenges us in both its collective and individual manifestations, and it accomplishes nothing to dwell on blame. We need to hear the stories of individuals and not distance ourselves from specific pain, but we also need to understand poverty as a gross dysfunction of our economic and political system.

Chapter Three

POVERTY AS A SERIES OF VICIOUS CIRCLES

etaphors are not meant to be interpreted rigidly, so that each symbol has only one referent. Rather, a metaphor is like a crystal that refracts light in different directions as you turn it. The stone in the Lazarus story is such a crystal.

For one poor family the stone might be a particular barrier such as the lack of a safe, decent, affordable place to live, or successful medical treatment, or access to transportation and affordable day care so that a parent can get to a job paying a livable wage. Roll away the particular stone(s), and the family climbs out of poverty on their own steam. All that some poor families need is an opening, and they can take it from there.

Persistent poverty, however, is both more than and different from a single problem, or even a combination of identifiable problems. Persistent poverty has a structural context that goes beyond specific circumstances that can be readily "fixed" with short term outside help and/or better decisions. Take the case of the tangible and powerful barriers of language and culture.

TEEGIE

In her pathbreaking book *Way With Words,* Shirley Brice Heath lays out the enormous chasm in development between mainstream and non-mainstream children, drawing upon her studies of two low-income communities in the Piedmont region of the Carolinas. One was a white community, steeped for four generations in the life of the textile mills, and the other a black community steeped in farming, but whose current members work in the mills. She shows how the economic and social isolation of both these low-income communities is embedded in their "way with words," which differs from that of the mainstream townspeople, both black and white.[1]

The issue is not native ability or intelligence, but cultural formation. Children from minority cultures are truly dependent upon a teacher, a relative, or another friendly adult recognizing and respecting the child's dilemma of cross-cultural communication, and patiently opening the world of mainstream language so the child can bridge his or her isolation.

Differences are shaped in the home and cultural community, developing from the way adults communicate with each other and with their children.

The major differences are in the styles of child rearing and verbal and nonverbal communication.

Heath says that among the townspeople—both black and white—adults speak directly to children from infancy on. In Trackton (the low income black community), adults constantly hold small children, passing them back and forth between them in the midst of a conversation, but talk *about* the children and rarely address them directly. Children thus acquire language and knowledge of adult ways mostly by observation and imitation rather than by face to face instruction.

She spells out the short- and long-term outcome of these differences. She notes that townspeople carried with them, as an unconscious part of their self-identity, numerous subtle norms, habits, and values, learned in childhood, about reading, writing, and speaking about written materials. They came to accept retrieval of the structure and information of written texts as critical to the presentation of form and content in their oral communication.

In school, they found continuity in these patterns of using oral and written language. Once on the job, they met these now thoroughly familiar tasks again, and they achieved success in their professions by displaying their skill at performing these tasks. In banks, stores, insurance offices, churches, the tennis and swimming clubs, and the mill's executive offices, they found these ways institutionalized. Throughout their home, school, and work lives, successful interactions depended on being able to talk from and with pieces of writing that were integral to appropriate interpretation of ongoing events. When their own children were born, they began to follow the parenting script they had learned in childhood, secure in their own success and comfortable with the roles and the lines.

For the children of Trackton and Roadville (low-income black and white communities), however, and for the majority of the millworkers and students in Piedmont schools, the townspeople's ways are far from natural. Indeed, they seem strange, and communication is a problem on both sides. The following exchange between teacher and student illustrates the complexity of the problem.

"The class was participating in 'sharing time' on the topic of pets, and the teacher called on Teegie: 'What kind of pet do you have?' Teegie answered, 'A dog, a big ol' collie dog. He been stay down my grandmamma house.' The teacher asked: 'Has he run away?' Teegie hesitated and answered, 'No, I been had 'im der.'"[2]

Later, the teacher told Shirley Brice Heath that she thought from Teegie's answer that he had not understood her follow-up question, and she was not certain what Teegie had meant. Heath responded that Teegie had understood and gave a rational explanation. She explained that his use of *been* in the first answer indicated that the keeping of his dog at his grandmother's house began in the distant past, and that he was using *stay* as a synonym for *live*. Thus Teegie had indicated in two ways that the dog had been gone a long time and that the dog lived at his grandmother's house. In his follow-up answer, Teegie reaffirmed this point.[3]

This small episode represents a major challenge in the increasingly diverse black, white, yellow, brown, multi-language American society. Here is a small child doing his best to participate fully in classroom discussion. If his thoughtful contribution is not understood, or worse, laughed at, his tendency will be to withdraw and withhold his self-expression and miss out on the possibilities of growth that manifest through self-expression perhaps more than in any other way. Unfortunately, very, very few teachers are trained to recognize and work with cultural differences.

In an agricultural or even an industrial-based economy, a different way with words, while limiting, does not foreclose the future. However, in an information-based economy the ability to communicate verbally and in writing is indispensable , and those who lack these essential skills are shut out of the mainstream. It is no wonder then why children raised in cultural isolation have such propensity to anger and despair, as reflected in the following story.

MARCUS

Nine-year-old Marcus saw Tom Lewis' car drive up. Within minutes, he and 10 other neighborhood children were on Tom's doorstep waiting for his community center to open. Tom, a retired African American policeman and my former colleague on the staff of For Love of Children, rents a two-story row house in one of the poorest and most dangerous neighborhoods in Washington, DC, for what he calls his "fishing school." He chose that name from the adage that if you give a person a fish, he will have a meal, but if you teach him to fish, he will eat for a lifetime.

Initially, Tom spent several nights a week hanging out at the house, after he finished his regular job at FLOC, available to talk with whomever would come by. His friends on the police force told him that he was crazy to go into that area alone. Tom replied, "This is where the children who need the most attention live. If they can't find us, we've got to find them."

On this particular evening Tom had brought a friend, a successful businessman who had grown up in the neighborhood, to talk with the kids who showed up. The children were impressed by his spiffy clothes and came up close to touch the fabric. The visitor took the cue and said, "When I was your age, I was very poor and all I had were second-hand clothes. My mother and my teachers told me that if I stayed in school and worked hard, I could get a good job someday, and buy any clothes I wanted. I listened to what they said. Now I have a good job, and I wear these clothes to work. If you listen to your mothers and teachers, you can do what I have done."

Marcus was not impressed. He broke in, "Mister, all that sounds real good for you, but we're not going to live that long. We're going to get shot."

The two adults were stunned, and so close to tears they turned away to hide their feelings. Marcus coolly turned his attention to the nearby pool table, and challenged another child to play. The other children knew that if they beat Marcus he was likely to have a tantrum and start a fight. This was how he let out his emotions.

Marcus lived next door in a "crack house" which he shared with his mother, grandmother, younger sister, two other adult women, and their four children. The crack house operated 24 hours a day. One of the four women was always up and available to sell drugs to customers. Some nights the customers outside the house were so thick Tom had to wade through a crowd to open his community center. Because of the drug trade the sound of gunfire is frequent in that neighborhood.

A few months later Marcus' mother was arrested and jailed, and the crack house was closed. Marcus' grandmother took Marcus and his little sister to an apartment a few blocks away. Marcus kept coming back to Tom's community center. During that year he learned to play games without fighting when he lost. A year later he was playing team sports in the city recreation league. He joined in the post-game ritual of congratulating opposing players, even when his team lost. Seeing this change of behavior, Tom sensed a small opening in a seemingly closed circle.

The odds against Marcus staying alive, staying out of jail, and reaching adulthood able to compete and ready to contribute are awesome. Among Marcus' peers, police arrest is a rite of passage. Many African American teenage boys identify with the prison system even more than their school, as is evident in the fad they adopted of wearing their trousers halfway down their buttocks. It reflects the frequency with which the police make them "spread eagle" as they pat them down for weapons or drugs. This fad is an "in your face" statement that has been picked up by suburban white boys to express their own adolescent rebellion.

For Marcus and his peers, however, death at an early age is still only one scenario, one possibility. It is not the only possibility, but at the present time it is the one that is most real to poor, minority youths like Marcus, the one that is shaping how they see their lives and future—as a closed circle.

SELF-FULFILLING PROPHECIES

My friend Dr. Beverly Coleman-Miller used to work for the District of Columbia Health Department. One of Dr. Coleman-Miller's responsibilities was to check every homicide that came into the city morgue for cause of death and to develop a profile for departmental reports. The majority of the homicides were attractive, able-bodied black males in their late teens and twenties. In many cases there were old wounds, generally around the knees—presumably a warning. In these cases the bullet holes that later killed were frontal, in the genital area and the chest, often from automatic gunfire.

Drug-related killings have become like an epidemic in many American cities. As a good public health official, Dr. Coleman-Miller began to look for clues to the epidemic. One day she started a conversation with a group of young black men resting from a basketball game on a neighborhood playground. When she asked how they saw the future, one 16-year-old answered, "My goal in life is to live to age 20, live good, and not get tortured."

"These young men see life in the same way as a terminally ill cancer patient," she told me. They have bought the story that American society is closed to them, and there is nothing they can do about it. These youngsters are terminally ill, to the extent that they adopt a cultural story that says they have no future, and that normal long-term considerations like job, career, marriage, and raising children don't apply to them.

The "death at an early age" story is not the only option. Many inner city youths living in the same neighborhoods and walking the same streets are living out a different story. A fundamental task for Tom Lewis and others who work with young people is to involve them in experiences that create alternative life-shaping stories. This is what Jesse Jackson is getting at when he leads high school assemblies in the chant, "I am somebody!" However, for that chant to mean anything, youths must have experiences in which they experience themselves as gifted and contributors to their communities and the wider culture. This means that as far as poverty and cultural isolation are concerned, attempting to rescue children one by one is ultimately futile. We must address these problems systematically in ways that generate possibility and change for whole neighborhoods as well as racial and ethnic groups.

STARTING FROM THE FUTURE

Cultural stories and experiences shape consciousness, and consciousness recreates itself in life. We are engaged in a battle for the minds and souls of America's children that both involves and transcends single problems like housing, health care, jobs, and education. As breakdown spreads through the systems our society relies upon for maintaining some semblance of fairness and social harmony, the urgency of institutional, community, and societal transformation intensifies. A critical distinction in this conversation for social transformation is between open systems and closed systems. A second crucial distinction is between existence generated by the past and existence generated from the future.

Our culture programs us to think that individual and social betterment is accomplished by skillfully building on the past. According to traditional thinking, we learn, expand, and grow by building on our experience, our education, our upbringing, our successes and failures. How we succeed in the present and what we see as possible in the future are largely determined by how effectively we build on the past.[4]

That way of thinking, however, is burdensome for children like Marcus. For them the past does not evoke energy. Their guiding stories are largely stories of resignation. Prolonged, unrelieved exposure to poverty and violence are deadening. Energy comes from aspiration and living out our aspirations.

Dr. Hope Hill, Professor of Psychology at Howard University, spends part of her time doing research with an inner city neighborhood mental health service for children. Her research has examined the consequences for children who witness violence in the community or at home and children who are repeatedly exposed to hearing about violence. Both direct witnessing and constant hearing about violence negatively affect the cognitive and emotional development of children. Dr. Hill says that 80% of the stressors identified in work with these children relate to homicide. In the community at large, few children who witness or constantly hear about violence receive attention to help them process the experience. Furthermore, research shows that children who witness violence are at higher risk than their peers of being victims and of committing violence.

Dr. Hill's goal is to break open this vicious circle of first- and second-hand victimization. She says that while we now have considerable clarity about the stressors, our task is to look at protection and protectors. Violence is a learned behavior. It can be supplanted. One protector is heavily values-oriented education with an African philosophical base. Another is an adult willing to make a commitment to a child throughout his/her childhood as a special friend, mentor, supporter, and model. The role of the protector is to stand in a future of possibility for the child and support the child in risking for that future.

Marcus' mother is out of jail now, after a year away from the family. She and her children are living with the grandmother, who is on public assistance.

Marcus' father lived in suburban Maryland. He would drop by every couple of weeks to check on the children. Sometimes he left them spending money, and always an exhortation to be good and work hard in school. Recently he died, reportedly of AIDS.

Marcus looks around him and sees mostly a closed, predictable world. The paramour of one of the women who lived in the crack house was murdered. Marcus knew who did it. Most of the older boys in his neighborhood carry guns—for self-protection, and in case someone "disses" (disrespects) them. It's all part of becoming a man on the street.

Increased funding and more youth programs are badly needed, but to be effective they must engage these youths in creating alternative cultural and personal stories. Our mainstream culture also needs new stories. Mainstream political thinking is largely pain-driven or problem-focused. It is fixated on talking about what's wrong, who is to blame, and offering a solution that will correct the wrong better than those responsible for the problem. This is the result of always starting from the past. What we need is the fresh air of possibility, the energy of vision, and the discipline of scaling compelling visions down to specific plans of action that move us toward the outcomes that we want. American society has this in common with Marcus and his peers: getting to a better future requires breaking out of old molds and accustomed ways of thinking and being, and daring to grow a future that is unrecognizable from the assumptions of the past. Most Americans can still get by for now through building on the past, although this is changing even as I write. The occurrence of breakdown in the systems we have traditionally relied upon to handle public responsibility, from foster care to police protection, is increasing faster than we can patch the holes. We must learn how to take quantum leaps not just in creating interesting projects but in evolving better systems. When one individual is functionally illiterate or otherwise unable to work, it is a personal tragedy. When millions of young people are only marginally employable, our nation is in very serious trouble.

ANOTHER CHILDHOOD

As I think about Marcus and his generation, my own childhood flashes into mind—how it was similar to and different from Marcus' experience. I was nine years old when Pearl Harbor was bombed and the U.S. declared war on Germany and Japan. To a child moving into adolescence, the war felt interminable. It was always there defining limits—gasoline rationing, food rationing, the call to postpone gratification and to support the war effort through purchasing war bonds. In the background was grief at the loss of those who would not be coming back and fear of who would be next. Violence was very much in the picture, but in a way that was partially understandable—to save the world from domination by the evil Hitler. Children and adults who lost loved ones were helped to grieve their loss by pastors and friends. Fallen victims were declared heroes, and their deaths were interpreted as the ultimate sacrifice for preserving freedom. If we used this language with Marcus, he wouldn't know what we were talking about.

When I was 14, sitting in the high school stadium watching a softball game, I heard the announcement that Japan had surrendered. The violence had ended. There would be no invasion of Japan. My oldest brother, Rumsey, who was waiting with infantry troops in the Philippines for that invasion, would be coming home. Rationing would soon be over. My heart leapt for joy. A huge stone had been rolled away, and my world was now open.

Before World War II there was another ordeal—living through the Great Depression. I was born in 1932 to middle class, college educated parents. Poor children went barefoot and middle class children like my brothers, my sister, and me wore good hand-me-down clothes shared between and within families. My father was a partner with his father in a retail lumber business. Business was so slow they were barely able to pay interest on the bank loan that kept the business afloat.

One day the bank announced that they were foreclosing the loan. The news was terrifying. However, instead of giving up hope, Dad and Granddad drew upon their connections. A crucial intervention by the bank president in a neighboring town caused the local bank to extend the loan. Hearing my father recall this incident over the years reinforced a basic cultural story of my upbringing that despite war, hard times, and other threats, the world is basically a friendly place.

THE WORLD OF HUGH BUMPHUS

My world as a child was very different from that of Hugh Bumphus, a black man who had worked summers with my father in a tobacco factory when they were teenagers. Granddad had sent his two children to Georgetown College in Kentucky. Dad returned to work in the family business. He eventually took over, then turned the business over to my oldest brother, who now shares ownership with his two sons.

Hugh Bumphus, on the other hand, never had a chance to get off the bottom and pass on opportunity to his children. Although he was respected for his character and considered an excellent worker, Hugh never earned more than a few cents above the minimum wage because of his race. Dad and Hugh's relationship as teenage friends changed to boss and colored employee when my father took over the family business.

Hugh had many skills. He knew, Dad knew, and everybody knew that were it not for segregation he could match anybody as carpenter or bricklayer and earn a wage that would have enabled him to own his own home and send his kids to college. But that was not to be. It would take two more generations for the world to be open to opportunity for Hugh's people, the way it had always been open for my family.

When I was a child, white adults were constantly telling me that "colored" people were satisfied with their lot except when damn Yankees, like union organizers, came south and stirred them up. One day when I was 10 years old, I heard the other side. I had persuaded my father to hire me as waterboy during the construction of a movie theater in the neighboring town of Hopkinsville, KY. The truck that transported us to and from "Hoptown" was desegregated. A white carpenter drove with the job foreman in the cab. In the back were white skilled laborers, black so-called unskilled laborers, my brother Rumsey Jr., who was an unskilled laborer, and me, the waterboy.

I enjoyed the banter of these men and the affection they displayed toward me, particularly my special mentor, Hugh Bumphus. My job as waterboy was to make rounds with my bucket of cold water to the various stations where the bricklayers, mortar makers, carpenters, and footing diggers were working. The whites insisted that I carry two cups, for exclusive use according to race, even though I dipped the cups out of the same bucket. The head bricklayer, in particular, regularly questioned me as to which cup was for whites and which for "coloreds," to make sure I followed the drill.

One day when the movie theater was nearing completion, I walked into a basement room where Hugh and three other black men were working and having a heated discussion. Bob, the youngest, was speaking to the older men with great animation, "The good Lord is not going to let this situation go on forever!" The older men nodded their heads. When they looked up and saw this 10-year-old white son of the boss waiting to offer them water, they became silent. They accepted the water, and after a pause resumed the conversation. In that moment I understood that what white adults were telling me about how black people saw the world was untrue. Segregation was a very bad deal for black people, but at that time their options were to endure the system or to move north and take on another set of problems.

CONTINUING SEGREGATION

It is now 50 years later, and although legalized segregation has been outlawed and repudiated, Marcus is growing up in a world as closed and segregated as that of Hugh Bumphus. Even though the civil rights movement opened doors for any grandchildren of Hugh Bumphus who had the skills to compete, Marcus' world is as closed as Hugh's. Race is one factor; an even greater factor is a dramatically changed economy which no longer provides the traditional stairsteps out of poverty that existed during the post-World War II industrial era. But race and economic change are not the whole of it.

The larger problem is the lack of a unifying social vision. Where a unifying vision is lacking, the consequence is the fragmentation of society into special interests working at cross purposes, where the strong get what they want by sacrificing access by the weak to the critical minimums they need to be self-sustaining. Without a larger vision to manage competition, we get a destructive Social Darwinism which makes desperate poverty unavoidable for those with the least power.

THE INNER CITY AS A WAR ZONE

Marcus and millions of other children are growing up in chaotic families and neighborhoods that have become virtual war zones. I recently learned this firsthand. On a cold January night in 1991, my wife and I had been watching a news update on Operation Desert Storm when we heard the staccato pop of automatic gunfire in our inner city neighborhood. I said to Sherrill, "That sound didn't come from the TV."

Sherrill and I live in a restored Victorian rowhouse in a racially and economically mixed neighborhood in Washington, DC, a mile northwest of the Capital, and a mile west of where Marcus lives. We went to the front door to look out. The street was empty. There was an eerie stillness, as though the whole neighborhood was holding its breath. Gradually people began coming out into the streets, a few at a time and then in a flood. Within minutes the whole neighborhood, it seemed, had gathered at the west corner of the block around a profusely bleeding, still breathing African American male in his twenties.

Sherrill, a social worker, knelt beside the young man. His eyes were fixed in a blank stare, as though he was walking an inner tightrope. A neighbor warned firmly, "Don't touch him!" Apparently he had been at such a scene before. Sherrill and I had not. The silence was penetrated by the shrill sirens of arriving police cars followed by an ambulance. The police quickly cordoned off the area, as the medics worked over the victim, loading him onto a stretcher and into the waiting ambulance.

Evidence of automatic gunfire remained in the large bullet holes in the trunk of the parked old-model Cadillac and the smashed church bulletin board at the corner. A neighbor looking out his second floor window had seen a man in a ski mask with an automatic weapon firing upon a man who was running for his life. When the victim fell, the murderer ran out of the lighted street intersection and quickly disappeared from sight. Another drug killing.

As we straggled back to our houses, I heard the undeclared war in the streets of our country scream for recognition—a war in which more young Americans would die that month in Washington, DC alone than in the Middle East. Multiply the violence in this one city by the escalating warfare in cities across the country, and the scale of the problem becomes apparent: black, brown, yellow, and white young men killing one another over claims to status, power, and scarce resources.

Washington, DC is in peril of dying as a great city. The tourists, lobbyists, and members of Congress will be the last to notice its demise. Profound and powerful forces are shaking and remaking this city, as they are every other large city in the United States. The population of the nation's capital is declining. It declined by 30,000, or 5%, in the decade of the 1980s and by another 17,000, almost 3%, in only two years from 1990-92.

The population in the wealthier, predominantly white part of the city, west of Rock Creek Park, is stable and growing modestly. East of Rock Creek Park population drops as increasing numbers of black middle class families move to the suburbs in search of better schools, better services, more affordable housing, safer streets, and lower taxes. The District of Columbia citizens who are staying put are in four classes: 1) the nonworking poor who are primarily welfare, unemployment, and disability recipients; 2) the working poor, whose incomes are close to minimum wage; 3) retirees on fixed incomes; and 4) white-collar professionals with mid to high salaries.[5]

If present trends continue, the population of the District of Columbia is likely to drop from 650,000 to 500,000 residents, of whom 200,000 will be supported by public assistance and 270,000 by modest wages or fixed incomes. If things stay the same, most of the tax burden will rest on the 30,000 residents— about 6%— with household incomes of $50,000 or more. At that point the nation's capital will join other large cities such as Philadelphia, St. Louis, Chicago, and Cleveland with large areas of boarded-up housing and miles of boarded-up commercial strips. Public safety will decline even further, and police, court, and incarceration costs will preempt the city's ability to turn the situation around.

The above decline in the tax base of the District of Columbia, alongside many other structural problems that were created by trying to hold on to the status quo in the face of the need for innovation, has led to the U.S. Congress turning over city financial control to an independent board appointed by the President. As the control board works with the city administration to downsize and reform government operations, the opportunity exists to engage the problem as a possibility. For example, underutilized, undervalued resources like vacant inner city land and boarded-up buildings represent opportunity. They are cheap to acquire, and you don't have to displace anyone.

Children like Marcus, whose homes offer very limited encouragement, require more intensive investment than children from stable families and neighborhoods. Moreover, each time the closed circle gets opened, the possibility is created of shifting a liability to an asset. The bottom line is enabling people and neighborhoods to become active in their own development. This can lead to the growth of new stories to supplant the despair of the past.

Chapter Four

SAYING NO TO CYNICISM, YES TO POSSIBILITY

Theologian Max Stackhouse says that freedom means there is a third choice, whatever the circumstances. I think Stackhouse is on to something very important for thinking about change, such as: When is change possible? What are the core elements that cause change to happen?

When I try to reduce my vision for my life's work into a single word what comes up is freedom—freedom for children, freedom for overburdened families, freedom for myself and all of us to shape our own destiny. This means that whatever the current state of affairs, whatever life throws at us, there is a third choice beyond the proverbial "between a rock and a hard place."

One characteristic that I observe in working with persons who have suffered prolonged deprivation in their lives either as children or as adults is the tendency to oscillate between two ways of thinking: despair and magic. The "death at an early age" story so characteristic of many young, inner city African American males reeks of despair. As these youths see it, their life choices are either to play by the rules of mainstream society in a game which is stacked against them, or identify with rebellious peers in making up their own rules and live boldly in the face of jail or death. They don't appear to have on their mental screens that there could be a third choice which could introduce more rewarding possibilities. On the other hand, many of these same youths switch in an instance to magical thinking and fantasize getting a big contract to play in the NBA. For many poor and nonpoor adults the magical thinking is winning the lottery.

Religion often plays a part in this too. If one is devout and compliant, or at least confesses his or her wrongdoing, God at some point is going to intervene and take away all this suffering. Meanwhile there is no plan of action to get from point A to point B. There is no commitment to change nor accountability. This is not sound teaching of any established religious tradition, but it is sadly widespread in American culture and very counterproductive. Authentic religious teaching says there is always a third choice besides despair and magic or despair and destructive rebellion.

What is it like for a child or adult to experience having a third choice that is neither fearful compliance nor destructive-to-others and ultimately self-defeating rebellion? This is freedom—the freedom to push back one's boundaries of knowledge, experience, and relationships, to act in one's own interest without doing violence to someone else.

The primary condition of the powerless, whose stories we have heard in previous chapters, is to be "out of the loop." They are, by and large, isolated, unaware of, unable to use, or cut off from opportunities that lead to developing their potential and to thriving. Possibilities may exist, but when people are out of touch with possibility in the world and in themselves, resignation takes over their psychic and spiritual space. When this occurs there is no ground for substantive change. Resignation, giving up on the possibility of breakthrough to a better future, is not confined to the persistently poor. It is appallingly evident in the mainstream too. Institutions and systems set up to protect and rescue children and assist families in crisis are often as dysfunctional, sometimes more so, than the families they serve. A common malady among people who stay very long in dysfunctional institutions is intellectual and spiritual resignation, because they cease to see a third choice between compliance and what looks like futile rebellion and even professional suicide. Indeed there is a widespread tendency for managers and workers to retire while still on the job, holding onto the pay and security until they are eligible for official retirement.

Georges Bernanos in *The Diary of a Country Priest* describes his parish in language that could equally apply to the modern human service bureaucracy. "My parish is bored stiff; no other word for it. Like so many others! We can see them eaten up by boredom, and we can't do anything about it. Some day perhaps we shall catch it ourselves—become aware of the cancerous growth within us. You can keep going a long time with that in you."[1] Bernanos calls the malady boredom. I call it resignation. It is believing that there is little or nothing we can do to cause change that will make a difference. We can't see or trust ourselves to risk a third choice. This stance does lead to boredom, and it directly affects the capacity of mainstream America to initiate the changes needed to open the tomb to a better life for poor children and their families. The issue of freedom applies both inside and outside the tomb.

On the Sunday before Martin Luther King, Jr. was assassinated in Memphis, I heard him speak at the Washington Cathedral. I will never forget seeing him lean over the pulpit and say with both force and compassion to that largely white audience, "You cannot be all that you can be until I can be all that I can be; and I cannot be all that I can be until you can be all that you can be." We must have that spirit of commonality to really help the poor. We have the freedom to help one another and exercising that freedom leads to greater freedom. The possibility of breakthrough to a different future shows up when we exercise our freedom to realize a shared vision.

In Chapters Five and Six, I will tell a story of a break-through in one system in one city—how a grass roots movement in the District of Columbia catalyzed the replacement of a 900-bed children's institution with community based alternatives. This story is an example of ordinary citizens exercising their freedom in ways that opened doors and carved stairsteps out of poverty for hundreds of children and families. But before getting to that story, I want to examine further the spiritual stones of resignation and cynicism within the privileged that must be rolled away to clear the way for the spread of freedom into the tomb. What we are exploring is not solely about helping individuals lift themselves out of poverty, but opening up the tomb of poverty as a widespread and intergenerational condition. This requires removing the spiritual blockages of resignation, cynicism, and withholding, as well as the structural barriers these attitudes reinforce.

THE OVERCOMING OF RESIGNATION IN THE LAZARUS STORY

The story of Lazarus contains the basic elements of a process that leads to transformation, both of the persistently poor and the rest of the community. "Roll away the stone" is Jesus' first charge to the community. Jesus brings the vision of a different future. His willingness to stand in that future and act to manifest it in the face of no understanding or agreement generates possibility.

Goethe once wrote, "Until one is committed, there is hesitancy, the chance to draw back, always ineffectiveness. Concerning all acts of initiative (and creation), there is one elementary truth—the ignorance of which kills countless ideas and splendid plans: that the moment one definitely commits oneself, then

Providence moves, too. All sorts of things occur to help one that would never otherwise have occurred. A whole stream of events issues from the decision, raising in one's favor all manner of unforeseen incidents and meetings and material assistance, which no man could have dreamed would have come his way."

When the Lazarus story begins, the community sees itself as powerless, and everyone knows that Lazarus is powerless inside the sealed tomb. The community can only see what it is accustomed to seeing. When you die, you're dead, and that's the end of it. In this extreme situation the community lacks the power and freedom to do anything but grieve. Its response is an example of resignation and cynicism to any possibility for newness.

But Jesus, the protagonist in the story, is not resigned. He creates in his mind a different future. With this vision in mind, he goes into action, pulling first the community, and, in turn, Lazarus, into action along with him.

Each completed step toward this unrecognizable future creates new possibility. When the stone is rolled away and Jesus calls into the tomb, Lazarus hears his name, and life begins to stir within him. Lazarus responds to the calling of his name, and takes what steps he can. His response creates possibility and leads to his unbinding. When the process is complete they all celebrate with a feast hosted by Lazarus. The vicious circle of decline and death, powerlessness and resignation has been opened into a circle of liberation.

In our reading of this story as a metaphor for today, the stone represents obstacles the persistently poor cannot move by themselves. It goes without saying that children cannot create schools that educate, or adequate health care, or a stable family. Schools, health care, and caring families must precede the children's response. People without access to capital cannot create jobs or affordable housing. Untrained people fail quickly in jobs requiring skills they have not developed or have no opportunity to develop. Disorganized people cannot exert the political clout to ensure their fair share of city services. For the poor to emerge from poverty on a broad scale, the larger community and nation must first remove the structural barriers that bar them from possibility. This requires collective action by those with the power to push aside structural barriers.

FROM VICIOUS CIRCLES TO LIBERATING CIRCLES

Persistent poverty as both an individual and societal condition manifests as a vicious circle. One problem attaches to another in a downward spiral. A member of the family has a chronic health condition. The need for medication takes money that is needed to pay the rent. A pipe bursts. A son gets in trouble with the police, which requires a lawyer. A family member is laid off. Notice of eviction. Go to the welfare office for help, which takes a day from work. Loss of pay. Etc., etc. Sometimes a good social worker helps the family break the spiral of problems into a series of manageable tasks, including getting temporary financial help. Things get better. But living as close to the edge as they do there is no cushion for the next time a small or large disaster strikes and sets off another downward spiral.

We must pay attention to individuals caught in vicious downward spirals. We, as local communities and as a nation, must also confront the big picture of the societal condition of persistent poverty as a vicious circle of negative reinforcing conditions and as embedded in a series of other vicious circles wherein each vicious circle reinforces and is reinforced by the others.

We must also notice the existence of a series of liberating circles alongside these vicious circles. These liberating circles also reinforce each other and collectively create a positive updraft in contrast to the downdraft of vicious circles. Looking at these vicious and liberating circles side by side makes it clear that any interruption of a vicious circle creates the beginning of a liberating circle. This, in fact, is what we mean by transformation—a fundamental shift in the flow of events and their impact.

Notice carefully the following diagram.[2]

FIVE VICIOUS CIRCLES THAT LEAD TO HOPELESSNESS, APATHY, VIOLENCE

FIVE LIBERATING CIRCLES THAT LEAD TO LIVELINESS, INITIATIVE, SAFETY

Poverty

Prison
Un/under employment
Poor diet
illness
No/unsafe housing
Crime
Drugs
Police
Courts

Forced Compliance

Remove safety net
Rejection by the privileged
Police oppression
Discipline by force
Child abuse
Teen violence

Racial and Cultural Alienation

Undeveloped skills
Compliance without choice
Loss of identity
Political manipulation

Pollution of Nature

Unchecked growth
Destruction of environment
Trash
Drugs
Petty Crime
Serious Crime

Senselessness and Godforsakenness

Unconscious death wish
Resignation
Despair
Drugs
Peace in dream worlds
Loss of purpose

Satisfaction of Material Needs

Decent housing
Nourishing diet
Health
Clothing
Job growth
Physical safety
Legal protection

Human Dignity Via Participation in Decision Making

Inclusion of child/family in decisions by helping institutions
Each voice counts
Distribution of political burden
Acceptance of political responsibility

Identity in the Recognition of Others

Fellowship
Self-respect
Self-Confidence
Productive working together
Encounter differences without anxiety

Cooperation with Nature

Diet
Exercise
Clean streets
Relationship to nature
Fun
Dance
Music
Beauty

Courage to Be, Freedom from Panic, Sense of the Whole

Security
Positive relationships with others
Trust
Will to live
Freedom
Peace

Theologian Jurgen Moltmann compares the vicious circle of persistent poverty to the physical process of dying. From a medical point of view, death is the endpoint of a vicious circle in which the basic relationships between the breathing, the brain, the heart and the circulation of the blood break down as the process of entropy runs its full course. The same occurs in persistent poverty, when people as individuals and groups confront closed systems of impenetrable barriers and negative feedback, which can cause the individual's or group's orientation on life to shift over to become an orientation on death. For this reason, Moltmann equates evil with vicious circles. He says, "The prayer of Jesus, 'And deliver us from evil,' is experienced and put into practice where men and women are liberated from these vicious circles, where the will to life is restored, and men and women come out of the rigor mortis of apathy and regain their life once more."[3]

TRANSFORMATION IS POSSIBLE

How can we begin to conceive quantum shifts from closed, vicious circles which create a huge downward suction to a series of liberating circles with an even more powerful updraft? Insights from modern physics may help. In contrast to current cynicism, which posits that the world is inexorably slipping downhill, chaos theory in modern physics tells us that we cannot predict where anything will be at any moment. We have to allow for particles continually interacting with one another, and know that when they do, new patterns often emerge. Reality is far more chaotic than we think, and, at the same time, there appears to be an underlying relationship between order and chaos. Old combinations of matter and motion break up and form new combinations.

This way of thinking is widely resisted by the cynical. Everybody "knows" that the past determines the future. If one's individual past doesn't do it, the collective past of the family, agency, company, town, race, nation, or human race will. Even the great Sigmund Freud said that he cured the miseries of the neurotic only to open him up to the normal misery of life.

Suppose, as an inquiry, we acknowledge that there is a fundamental distinction between future and past. One has already occurred, and the other does not yet exist except in our minds. If so, then the future is indeed open with unrecognizable possibilities, provided we can part with the past, and stand, think, speak, and act from a vision of a bold new future.

In the first three chapters of this book I have tried to give voice to the pain and injustice of a divided country in which the majority are so blessed with opportunity that most of us don't appreciate what we have, while a minority lack access to the critical minimum that is necessary for normal human growth and development—jobs, housing, education, health care, and personal psychological and physical safety. The root problem in this country, however, is not scarcity but resignation and the withholding of spirit, love, resources, and intelligence by both poor and comfortable. Furthermore, resignation is spiritually, morally, intellectually, and economically stifling.

Many people have concluded that the world is, at best, far too complex, and, at worst, far too evil for average citizens to accomplish anything at a community or societal level other than giving a helping hand here and there. These people are already resigned to our cities, our nation, and our world drifting downhill. Cynicism and resignation dominate their thinking and conversation, and there is ample evidence in the world out there to support their assessment.

Transformative thinking, the opposite of despair, resignation, and cynicism, is the embodiment of freedom. It requires us to engage with the inherent, unceasing conflict between vision—what we want—and reality—what we have. We will consider this subject in more detail in Chapters Nine and Ten. Our challenge at this point is to acknowledge the pain of the past without being pain-driven, and to shift our spiritual and intellectual weight to uncovering and identifying with our aspirations, until we become aspiration-evoked rather than pain-driven. This is a fundamental shift in consciousness and way of thinking. And it is absolutely critical for both personal and societal empowerment.

THE FUTURE IS OPEN

Amos Wilder once wrote that every story "posits a scheme or order in the nowhere of the world." In the last chapter, I described how the "death at an early age" story, for many minority youths, makes sense of the social chaos in which they find themselves, to the point that they withhold their life force from long-range goals such as developing a marketable skill, raising a family, and contributing to the betterment of their community.

These young people have invented a modern version of the ancient philosophy: "Eat, drink and be merry, for tomorrow we die." It is interesting that in living that story these youths project a John Wayne kind of rugged individualism that is as American as apple pie. They have adopted a profound American cultural image that has given millions of American males a mirror for identity, and put their own spin on it. Except this version ends with everyone getting shot. There are no longer good guys and bad guys, only the dominators and the dominated.

It is ironic that alienated youths are ideologically suiting up for the games of mainstream American male self-expression, even as they see themselves denied access to the playing field. African American youths would likely deny any affinity with John Wayne. Their heroes are the facile-tongued rap artists (not the lumbering "aw shucks" white frontiersman), the tough guys in the blacksploitation films, the black athletes who dance and profile in the end zone after scoring a touchdown, and the cool street dudes with spectacular clothes, spectacular cars, and spectacular women on their arms. Nonetheless, the swaggering, go-it-alone, "make my day" male cockiness is a constant. It just may be that aspiration to the heroic is part of the hard wiring in the male psyche. Like a stream, if it is blocked in its natural flow, it will cut a channel elsewhere.

Suppose, as an exploration, we apply ourselves to invent new hero and heroine stories that introduce a different scheme or order "in the nowhere of the world," and that open up positive and creative channels for self-expression. Suppose that we dare to reckon the future as open for everyone and look for stories or tell stories that shift the way youths see the world.

Matthew Arnold once said, "We are living between two worlds; one that has died and another that is struggling to be born." Suppose we tell our stories from this premise, noticing the vicious closed circles about us, but giving greater attention to the possibility and presence of liberating circles. Next, let us share with one another the excitement of what we see being born, as well as acknowledge the struggle of the birth process. Our stories, however, must be honest. No one leaps from poverty to highly paid, glamorous jobs in society without taking the myriad small steps that move them from one performance level to another.

TOWARD RACIAL AND CULTURAL INCLUSION

Teegie and Marcus in Chapter Three represent millions of American children who are on the cusp between a world that has died and another that is struggling to be born. Their going down with the old world or rising up with the new is in the most profound sense a factor of communication and self-confidence. The gift of language, the power to read and to communicate, is a ticket to the new world. Someone has to give them that ticket.

What about skin color? Skin color cannot be changed. With race it is not a matter of teaching skills but of changing the way white Americans respond to skin color. Educated African Americans have acquired the language that enables them to participate in the mainstream, but they still pick up a feeling tone in their places of business and residence that says, "If you're white, you're right; if you're brown, stick around; if you're black, stay back."

Feelings derive from the past. They derive from experiences and beliefs begun in childhood. Cynics who start from the past and stand in the past say that feelings about skin color are unchangeable. Those who look at life from the perspective of a world struggling to be born say that new reality can evolve.

Monica Jackson, an African American volunteer at a cultural diversity event, noticed that all six of the volunteer assistants for the event were black. Monica reports this conversation with herself. "I've been doing this assistant thing for about six months, and I keep thinking, 'Man, the only thing they'll let us black people do is run their [stuff] around so that they can do transformation, except I keep getting something out of it so I keep doing it. After this cultural diversity event I now know it isn't me thinking that white people are making me assist. It's black people talking through me, and I have no choice but to think that, because 200 years of people and tragedies are having me think this. And I, Monica, have more fun here than any place else. I can't wait to get here. I love serving people. Then the coolest thing was, the rest of my regular assisting team, none of whom were at the event, got it too. And something got heard and disappeared from over there with them that I hadn't heard, and I saw for the first time this conversation had shifted for them too and it was released. What has opened up is an awareness of the degree to which I am used by 'voices' that are not who I am, 'voices' that tell me how to be with other people as a group. The more I confront this, the more I see how large it is and the more free I am."[4]

A new future can only emerge as we, black, white, yellow, brown, poor, and comfortable, step back from the past and see it as the past and not necessarily the future. By making this fundamental distinction in thought and in practice, we clear space for new communication and new possibilities.

THE PARADOX OF PROGRESS

U.S. society appears to be evolving toward greater complexity and dynamism in some areas and regressing severely in other areas. In cities across the U.S., a regression is occurring in the quality of life, in the well-being of children, and most noticeably, in public safety, at the same time that millionaires, white, black, and other races, are multiplying. In parts of town where drug trafficking is open and brazen, the regression calls up the days of the wild West when men settled their differences with guns in place of reason. Today, many youths of all races who see no way to a rewarding future by the traditional routes are identifying with a subculture in which cleverness, quickness, weapons, and the nerve to use them get you what there is to be gotten. The U.S. faces the awesome contradiction of leading the industrialized world in both the production of wealth and the production of crime and persistent poverty.

Today, we confront an extraordinary range of problems and needs in our local communities and the nation at large. Old public systems, such as social services, schools, and health care, that we have counted on to meet community needs, are breaking down. Nonprofit organizations are being birthed daily to try to fill gaps in services. The nonprofits, in turn, bombard the already heavily taxed citizen with competing appeals for funding and volunteers. Everyone is asked to express their generosity, stand up and be counted, and engage in the struggle for a society that works for everyone. Persistent poverty and other social problems require complex, usually long-term responses, which are beyond the capacity of single individuals to sustain. Simple, straightforward needs that can be met by one act of assistance still occur, but complex needs that require leadership, coordination, and sustained involvement are the order of the day. Perhaps the most important helping skill today is knowing how "to work the system," to match need with opportunity. The problem is that teamwork within and between agencies and between public and private sectors is frequently lacking. Energy and money are wasted, and burnout runs high.

The breakdown of traditional systems and the shift of responsibility to nonprofits, however, is telling us something. The rise of nonprofit service and advocacy organizations says there are a lot of people who care and are putting their care into action by investing their time, energy, and money. The breakdown of traditional systems tells us that we are in crisis as a society. Crisis, however, is not necessarily bad. The Chinese word for crisis has two characters, one signifying change and the other opportunity.

Systems in crisis need to be rethought and redesigned. They are too slow. There are too many levels of control. The people closest to the action are disempowered. Communication gets stuck at the top, and lower levels don't know what the top level is up to. The only accountability is the threat of adverse media coverage. This must change.

Elizabeth O'Connor says in her book, *Inward Journey, Outward Journey,* that there are two simultaneous journeys involved in human transformation. One is interior work, and the other is the work of transforming the institutions, structures, and adverse conditions in the world. These two journeys feed each other, to the point that attempting one without the other will undermine both. An increasing number of people understand this as it applies to the individual. We must now go a step further and apply this insight to our organizations, institutions, and systems.[5]

THE INWARD JOURNEY

The inward journey is ageless and universal. It encompasses the continuous struggle between two sides of every person. It is the conversation between our generous side and our withholding side. A piece of the hard wiring of our humanity is the desire and need to contribute to the well-being of others. The totally self-contained person is dying or already dead. Just as there is a vicious circle of poverty, there is a vicious circle of riches. Statistics indicate, paradoxically, that as people rise in income, they tend to give away smaller and smaller proportions of their wealth. The reason is that most of us change our life-styles to match our incomes, so that the greater the income the more complex the life-style, which then requires escalating amounts of time, energy, and money to maintain. This is the case of a consumption-driven society which places highest value on possessions. When is enough enough? Why invest increasing amounts in possessions that give less satisfaction per investment the more we acquire? Which gives the greater return—acquisition or contribution to others and the world? Wealth can be a prison the same as poverty. They just look different.

This interior conversation occurs regardless of where one is on the economic scale. Everyone, from beggar to billionaire, struggles between sharing and withholding. Some with the least share the most freely. This never-ending interior conversation between generosity and withholding is projected onto the world, and what shows up out there is a direct reflection of the interior conversation. Examples of interior change manifesting in public change are the passage of child labor laws, the desegregation of schools, the current engagement with health care as a right rather than a privilege, and countless unsung one-to-one relationships such as foster parenting, adopting children with special needs, and standing by people dying of AIDS.

CHOOSING A WORLD WE LOVE

I have framed this book as an inquiry into the possibility of ordinary citizens in partnership with government and community institutions reinventing American society so that all children are empowered to develop into resourceful, contributing, and self-determining citizens who keep the process going for succeeding generations. This inquiry is about getting ahead of the curve.

Visitors to the U.S. from developing countries are initially unimpressed by American conditions of poverty. Their image of poverty is dirt streets, outdoor toilets, no running water, and tent-like housing made of odd pieces of wood, sheets of corrugated metal, and newspaper to cover the walls. Many Americans share this perspective, and they consider poverty in this country both tolerable and primarily the fault of the poor themselves.

Poverty in the U.S., however, is not the same as poverty in third and fourth world countries. Some African dialects have no word for poverty. There is insufficient distinction between rich and poor in those cultures to merit community attention because the whole village shares in scarcity in times of drought and in abundance when rain is plentiful. Poverty in the U.S. is fundamentally different. Rain can be plentiful, crops abundant, plants operating at full capacity, and children still go hungry (in all dimensions of that term) because of parental and societal abuse and neglect. A complex, technological economic system needs effective, accessible infrastructures to assist people who need help. Alongside the fundamental right to live are the right to be treated with respect and the responsibility to do what one can for one's self. Our task is to combine generosity, respect, and responsibility.

AN ANCIENT EXAMPLE OF
AN EFFECTIVE 'SAFETY NET'

Every society from the beginning of civilization has had to look out for the unprotected. The ancient Jews dealt with this dilemma through their understanding of covenant. All land, the means of production in an agricultural society, was understood to belong to God, and to be held in trust by those fortunate enough to have access to it. A fundamental condition for the continued use of the land was the responsibility to tend to the needs of the landless, who, in the Old Testament, are subsumed under the rubric of "widow, orphan, and refugee." These three groups represented all who lacked access to the means of independent survival and the production of wealth—that is, land. These foundational understandings were codified in laws believed to be given directly by God through Moses.

For example, the law of Moses taught that a farmer was obligated to leave the corner of his grain field unharvested so that the widow, the orphan, and the refugee could survive without having to beg. In harvesting figs, the farmer was permitted to shake the tree only once. The figs still hanging were to be left for the widow, the orphan and the refugee to harvest.[6]

Food was left for the poor to harvest. It wasn't delivered to their doors in bushel baskets. Gleaning was work. It combined generosity with respect and responsibility.

As that society evolved from a farming economy to a mercantile economy, these teachings were ignored, and the poor were reduced to begging. The Old Testament prophets, the conscience of society, were outraged at the spread of beggary and considered widespread destitution a telltale sign of rejection of the covenant by the whole nation, and a manifestation of sin. Poverty thus was a sign that the materially blessed had ignored the terms of the blessing, and the prophets held the prosperous accountable. According to the prophets, justice is measured by the well-being of groups with no protection other than what the whole nation assures. Moreover, the ancient Jewish prophets warned that the nation would be incapable of standing on its own with other nations whenever it turned its back upon the unprotected in its midst.

Diversity of ability, income, and opportunity seem to be built into the nature of things. The communist experiment to eliminate diversity has failed. Capitalism, as we now know it, is also found wanting. U.S. capitalism is surrounded by an intolerable amount of beggary, homelessness, intergenerational poverty, and the abuse and neglect of children. A new economic system that hasn't appeared yet will provide adaptive mechanisms that enable the whole population to be on the playing field. We can only imagine what that will look like.

An essential piece of our new shared vision is the example of advocacy by and for the physically challenged. They have made it very clear that they do not want pity. They want sidewalks with passageways so people in wheelchairs can cross the street under their own control. They want bus lifts and subway elevators that permit them to use public transportation. They want access to the opportunities and systems that are there for the majority, and they want to be acknowledged for their resourcefulness in coping with their disabilities. They do not want to be isolated from mainstream living. Things are moving toward a vision of inclusion for the physically challenged. The law is now on their side after centuries of neglect. We have a long way to go but we are moving in the right direction.

The same is true for the elderly. In the 1960s the greatest concentration of poverty in this country was among the elderly. In a genuine triumph of social policy, with the expansion of Social Security and the enactment of Medicare, elder poverty has been greatly reduced.

Now it is children who suffer the most from poverty. Among those under the age of six, one out of four lives in poverty as the government defines it, which in 1997 was no more than $16,400 for a family of two adults and two children. Among young children living in families headed by married couples, 13 percent were poor. But among young children in households headed by women with no spouse present, 66 percent were poor.

A 1993 study of 26 major U.S. cities found that as many members of families as single men were homeless, each representing about 43% of the total homeless population. In previous years members of families accounted for about a third of homeless people seeking help. Andrew Cuomo, Secretary of the U.S. Department of Housing and Urban Development, says that the families tend to be less visible than homeless singles because they often live in cars or makeshift shelters far from downtown streets. While many homeless singles suffer from mental illness or substance abuse, families tend to be victims of the lack of jobs and require different services.

Where do we start to implement a vision of inclusion for all children and all people? My answer is that we listen carefully to Jesus' command to roll away the stone, to notice where that command shows up for us, and start there. There is little that any one person can do alone to move entrenched barriers, but one person can recruit a few others, and 60 to 80 people working together can successfully tackle a complex community task. When a comprehensive alternative is not in view, it is important to look for starting points for critique and resistance and to stay involved for possibilities to manifest. The stone is moveable. It can be rolled out of the way so that others we are called to serve and we ourselves can gain access to a better life.

Part Two

ACTION: A SMALL CHURCH
TAKES ON A CITY GOVERNMENT
(A Modern Version of David Meets Goliath)

Chapter Five

CASE STUDY: THE FORMING OF FOR LOVE OF CHILDREN AS A STRUCTURE FOR COMMUNITY ACTION

T he previous chapters describe the virtually permanent economic, social, and spiritual segregation of poor children, youths, and families from the rest of the American population, if we do nothing. This kind of segregation is not based only on race; it includes whites and Hispanics, as well as African Americans and Native Americans. Without significant intervention, 10 percent and more of the U.S. population will live out their lives in brutal isolation from the rest of American society.

How can the connection be restored? What can make a lasting difference? Who will roll away the stone from their tomb of economic, social, and spiritual isolation?

In the Lazarus story, Jesus stands at the sealed-off entrance to the tomb and calls to the gathered people, "Roll away the stone!" Jesus asks the community of Lazarus' own family and neighbors for a response of co-creation. Something new is about to happen, and they are to be part of it. Freedom for Lazarus can't happen unless they do their part. If they do respond to the call, their visibly modest efforts will result in astounding change. Hesitantly, reluctantly, Lazarus' community responds. And they grumble.

"That body has been lying there four days and by now it stinks. This man is crazy. Why should we become involved? It's over, he's gone, it's hopeless. It's disgusting what he asks us to do." Nevertheless, at Jesus' prompting, they finally act. They push the heavy stone to the side, doubting all the while.

In the next two chapters I will tell a contemporary story of rolling away the stone of isolation. The story describes FLOC's origins in this chapter, and the successful struggle to close Junior Village in the following chapter. This story is a witness to how ordinary citizens can help persistently poor families and abused and neglected children be free; how the free community, outside the tomb, can help release the captives inside.

BACKGROUND

Following World War II, a wave of rural southern African Americans migrated north, looking for job opportunities in cities along the eastern seaboard—New York, Washington, Philadelphia, Baltimore, and in the midwest, Cleveland, Chicago, and Detroit. Washington, DC, a white collar city with no heavy industry, was not well supplied with the jobs they sought. Some of the new immigrants got government jobs, but many women and children ended up on the welfare rolls.

As the welfare rolls swelled, so did a conservative reaction in the U.S. Congress, which then governed the city. Senator Robert Byrd, the chairman of the Senate Appropriations Subcommittee, which controlled city finances, ordered a crackdown on "welfare cheaters" and strict enforcement of the "man in the house" rule, which prohibited public assistance to women and children if an able-bodied man lived with the family or was in regular contact.

As a result of this purge, 4,000 women and children were dropped from the public assistance rolls between 1962 and 1965. But what the city had not anticipated was the consequence—a dramatic increase in the number of children separated from their homes and placed in Junior Village, the city's front-end resource for out-of-home placement. Over that three year period the average daily population of Junior Village increased from 200 to over 900 children. Two stones were sealing the tomb now: restricting public assistance to families without fathers, and institutionalizing children whose families were unable to make ends meet.

In the spring of 1965 an event in another part of the country spoke the command, "Roll away the stone!" to a group of Washington, DC, clergy. Martin Luther King, Jr. called the clergy across the nation to join him in Selma, Alabama, for a demonstration to end racial segregation. The experience was so powerful that some of the participants described it later as a conversion. As the planeload of clergy from Washington, DC returned home, they committed themselves to become involved with the plight of the poor in their city, to roll away oppressive barriers as King and the Southern Christian Leadership Conference and other civil rights groups were doing across the south. Two concrete initiatives developed out of that commitment.

THE COALITION OF CONSCIENCE

One of King's lieutenants, Reverend Walter Fauntroy, pastor of the New Bethel Baptist Church, drew together a coalition of activist African American and white clergy, social workers, and church members to identify and challenge specific barriers that were blocking the poor. As their first target the coalition focused on restrictive city welfare policies, particularly the "man in the house" rule. Members developed a five-point campaign for improved welfare services:

1. eliminate the "man in the house" rule
2. increase public assistance grants for food and housing (Grants had not been adjusted in over eight years.)
3. reduce the staff of investigators of welfare fraud and increase the number of trained case workers

(Washington, DC had 58 investigators, three times the number of New York City.)

4.   strengthen foster care by raising board and care rates

5.   extend the city's day care program. (Although some 19,000 working mothers in the city had children under six, there were only four low-cost day care centers, with a total capacity of 185 children.)

Public rallies, marches, and lobbying over a six-month period generated considerable media attention, which was followed by revisions in the "man in the house" rule, increased city financial aid to families in crisis, and the establishment of a free temporary shelter for evicted families. The coalition stayed intact for about 12 months. During that year, which coincided with the launching of the federal "War on Poverty," the average daily population of Junior Village began to drop —from over 900 to 600 between 1965 and 1966.

THE BEGINNING OF FOR LOVE
OF CHILDREN (FLOC)

While the Coalition of Conscience focused on changes in welfare policy, another group formed to address the use of institutional care for all ages of homeless, abused, and neglected children. One of the clergy at Selma was Gordon Cosby, founder of the ecumenical Church of the Saviour in Washington, DC. When he returned from Selma, he committed an hour a day to meditate on both the Bible and the newspaper in order to discern a direction for himself in the freedom movement. One day, two items in the paper caught his eye. One was a story about one of the ten most wanted criminals in the U.S. This man, he read, had never had a home; he had been shunted from birth parent to foster homes and institutions until he was grown. The other story was about the overcrowding at Junior Village. It described army tents erected to handle the overflow of 900 children, half of them under six years old.

Cosby recalled stories told by members of his congregation who were regular volunteers at Junior Village. One evening they couldn't figure out why it took so long to bathe the children in the toddler cottage. Finally they noticed that as soon as a child got her bath and the hugging that went with being dried in a big towel, she or he would go to the back of the line for another bath. The volunteers then decided to powder the buttocks of the children as they were dried to keep track.

As Cosby thought about the way deprivation was structured into the very existence of this institution, Junior Village ceased to make any sense. The need was not for more volunteers or staff but for a different system. An institution like Junior Village was simply the wrong way to care for children. Children should be with their own parent(s), if possible, and if not, in foster homes and other small, homelike settings. As *Washington Post* writer J.W. Anderson later wrote, "Junior Village is a factory for mental retardation and mental illness." This institution must be closed and replaced with better alternatives.

SHARING THE VISION

The process turned out not to be much different than Jesus calling the doubting and bewildered onlookers to roll away the stone from Lazarus's tomb. Harking back to Selma, Cosby began to envision a broad, loose-knit social action movement by the metropolitan Washington religious community. Junior Village could be closed, Cosby reasoned, by mobilizing small dedicated groups of 5 to 10 people in Catholic, Protestant, and Jewish congregations in the area. If as many as 200 congregations formed these small groups, and each group relocated or prevented placement of five children, Junior Village could be virtually closed within a year.

Cosby shared his vision with his congregation and invited interested people to meet with him after the service. About 30 people stayed. They stayed the next Sunday and the next. Soon a planning group was formed and a number of tasks outlined.

One task was gathering information, reading all the material they could get their hands on so they could recruit others. Another task was to contact a minister or lay leaders in each of the 1,300 Catholic, Protestant, and Jewish congregations listed in the yellow pages. Over the next three months nearly 200 churches and synagogues sent pastor-lay pairs to a series of Sunday afternoon briefings.

Each minister and layperson was challenged to initiate a single, small, disciplined group who would meet weekly or bi-weekly to engage in an inward journey of mutual support and spiritual growth and an outward journey to address the needs of children and families in the city.

Through the summer of 1965, the Sunday afternoon briefings went on. Finally an ecumenical coordinating council was formed, consisting of the ministers of five participating churches. They first described themselves as the "Crusade for Children." When volunteer Kathryn Campbell proposed the name "For Love of Children" and the acronym FLOC, they immediately adopted it.

CREATING FOSTER HOMES

Though the groundswell of church initiative to relocate children from Junior Village or prevent placement did not materialize, a nucleus of 25 to 30 people kept at the task. Every Saturday morning they would canvas selected neighborhoods looking for prospective foster parents.

The Saturday morning meetings were a small rendition of the SCLC civil rights mass meetings—singing, prayers, sharing of experiences, a bit of preaching, and then the door-to-door canvases.

This weekly exercise attracted between 30 and 40 persons each Saturday morning, some regularly, others occasionally. During the 12 weeks of meetings, 138 foster parent applicants were found and the names turned over to the Department of Public Welfare (DPW). DPW was lax in processing the applications, so FLOC members confronted them with their seriousness about finding alternatives to Junior Village.

These initial activities were undertaken with entirely volunteer leadership, which soon became difficult to sustain. Yolande Ford, a member of the Church of the Saviour, was asked to serve as a half-time paid coordinator. Money for a salary and organizational expenses was pledged by the churches and individuals who had embraced the mission, and nonprofit corporation status was attained.

FINDING HOUSING FOR FAMILIES

Initially three groups formed, each helping two or three families with children in Junior Village or in foster care to regain custody of their children. Lack of housing was the initial stone to be rolled away, so the group concentrated on finding suitable houses or apartments. They needed a variety of homes for the variety of families they worked with.

One family consisted of a blind mother, a father who worked as a garbage collector and their four children. The parents lived in a basement with two of the children. Their home was one big room, with one 60-watt bulb overhead, a hot plate, and no refrigerator. The older two children, boys six and eight, were in Junior Village.

Two other families had six and eight children respectively, half of them in Junior Village or in foster care. All the parents worked, the mothers as domestics and the fathers on jobs like golf caddying or moving and hauling. Two years before, their children had gone into Junior Village after the families were evicted for arrears in rent. The parents couldn't get public housing or afford rents on the open market. While some of their children were in public custody the parents and the younger children lived with friends.

A fourth family group consisted of six siblings from ages 10 to 18 and no parent. They had been placed in Junior Village as a group when their mother died and their father disappeared. The children asked to be allowed to live together in the community. DPW granted their request on the condition that FLOC would arrange housing and provide close supervision. The plan worked for several months. When the younger children began missing school, FLOC volunteers took them into their homes with DPW approval and helped the siblings to do as much together as possible.

The mission groups dealt with housing on a case by case basis. It was cheaper in 1966 in Washington, DC, for FLOC to buy three- to four-bedroom houses and rent to the families than to rent decent, adequate space for families with six to ten members. A few churches and individuals made low or no interest loans to FLOC for down payments for the "Hope and a Home" effort. Piecing together 6% bank loans with these private loans, FLOC was able to rent whole houses to large families for $150 to $200 per month.

When FLOC was able to find appropriate housing for the families, the children returned from Junior Village with great rejoicing. But the reality of the day to day struggle for survival did not go away. FLOC was now acting as landlord, trying to get by on a shoestring budget. When families did not pay their rent, volunteers had to learn to be both supportive friend to the family and the landlord's representative.

RELATIONSHIPS BETWEEN
VOLUNTEERS AND FAMILIES

Somehow these friendships worked more often than they failed, perhaps because volunteers kept their focus on very tangible goals. Relationships were built by going with the parents to the police station for a child picked up for shoplifting, or helping parents deal with a medical problem, or getting tutoring for children with learning problems. Sometimes the most appreciated assistance was arranging times of family recreation at new places like a farm or the beach.

From the 10 families related to FLOC in its first two years, none of the 40 children had to return to Junior Village. But it was always challenging to maintain these supporting friendships and help keep the families together.

Muriel Lipp, a FLOC volunteer, described in her journal her group's involvement with a family.

"June 28, 1967: This week our group, Cindy Lehman, Kathrene Lawson and I went to the shelter for homeless families and met Ramona and Larry Smith [name changed] and their two daughters. They've been living in their car for two weeks. They are out of money, and Larry is laid off from his job.

All of them are thin and undernourished. Kathrene offered to let them move in with her, and FLOC paid her a little money for food and emergencies.

June 30, 1967: We tried to encourage Larry to pursue two possible jobs he says could be lined up. But Ramona is not working out at Kathrene's. She just sits around and smokes cigarettes. Kathrene has been paying some of the food money for Ramona to get Vitamin B-12 shots from her own private doctor. She also gets nerve pills (tranquilizers) from him. This costs $20 per week. We agreed this knocked the budget for a loop. We will visit her doctor, who doesn't take Medicaid, and ask about her situation.

July 14, 1967: Several days ago Ramona and Larry and the children left Kathrene's house because we wanted the babies checked at the Jubilee Clinic. The Smiths are afraid Welfare will see the children and take them away. (Ramona, in a previous marriage, had two other children taken away from her.) Anyway, they sneaked off.

A couple of days later they came back. Ramona looked worse than ever. She'd had a seizure of some kind. We're wondering if she is epileptic.

August 2, 1967: Today we met and decided on our priorities:

1. The children's health
2. Ramona's health
3. Temporary care for children while parents get health back, a job started and an apartment.

The big object is to try to rehabilitate this family without separating the children too much from the parents. We will get a friendly doctor to intervene in case they report neglect of the children at the hospital and seek to take them away.

Kathrene is willing to have Larry and the children continue to live with her as long as necessary, but she refuses to care for Ramona. Ramona orders her around and does nothing to help herself or others.

How do we get Ramona to care for herself? She absolutely refuses to go to the hospital or a clinic. She wants only her own doctor and her tranquilizers. We may have to tell her if she doesn't cooperate, we can't continue.

August 9, 1967: Ramona allowed FLOC to place the children in a private home in Arlington, VA, where the Smiths could visit at any time.

The babies began to gain weight, Ramona's health was being monitored, and Larry was job hunting.

One day the Smiths came out to the home to visit their children, and Ramona took the children, saying they didn't want anything more to do with FLOC.

That was the last we heard of the Smiths."

Not all the attempts to help families worked out as volunteers hoped, for the families were confronted with multiple problems, compounded by their fear of the system and fear of change.

FLOC volunteers learned a lot in the process, a lot about the complexities of rolling away stones, and a lot about power and powerlessness and charity and justice. Many of the families they worked with during this time took hold and began to reconstruct their lives together.

Chapter Six

SUCCESS AND CONTINUING CHALLENGES

I n 1966, after a busy and productive initial year, the coordinating council governing FLOC concluded that unless the organization hired a full-time director and began recruiting new members, it would die. A committee got a $5,000 grant from the Public Welfare Foundation, matched by another $5,000 in pledges from churches and individuals, to hire a full time executive director.

The announcement that FLOC was looking for an executive director made my heart beat faster. I was 34, a FLOC volunteer, and previously a Baptist pastor in the suburbs of Washington. Drawn to the Church of the Saviour, I had resigned my pastorate the year before and got a job with a DC government job training program for unemployed heads of households in order to learn first-hand the principles and work of the Church of the Saviour. Through the job training program I became acquainted with families who had children in Junior Village. When I was offered the FLOC job in the summer of 1966, with a budget of $10,000, an office and telephone provided by the Church of the Saviour, a free bookkeeper, and no secretary, I started my own Abrahamic journey toward the land I trusted God to show me.

After getting acquainted with the FLOC volunteers, visiting the four small groups then in operation, and meeting key Department of Public Welfare personnel, I set out to form additional mission groups. I decided to conduct a 12-week orientation course one night per week in a local church through the fall of 1966.

I found attorneys, social workers, and university professors to help me, since I had no professional training in social work or child welfare. I advertised the course in local newspapers and church bulletins, and 40 people showed up the first night.

Using my theological training, I opened each training session with a Bible study, focusing on a particular metaphor which had power for me. My first selection was Genesis 12: "Go from your country and your kindred and your father's house to the land that I will show you. And I will make of you a great nation, and I will bless you, and make your name great, so that you will be a blessing." For years, this call to Abraham had been ringing in my ears, and it described better than I could the kind of faith journey we were undertaking. Something, perhaps Someone, was stirring us to take up the cause of homeless children and their families. The obstacles and complexities were enormous, and we could not see ahead of time exactly what to do or how to do it. What we did see was the reality of the children and their families. And we believed that change could happen by following the leads we had, learning and adapting as we went, and persisting in the journey.

In addition to this kind of Bible study, the course covered both systemic and personal issues affecting poor multiproblem families, the structure of the social service delivery system, and the role of the courts in child abuse and neglect cases. Another key goal was to build community among the participants.

Three new groups formed as a result of that first orientation course. One, drawn from members of a Lutheran experimental ministry called the Community of Christ and their pastor, John Schramm, developed a group home for adolescent Junior Village girls. A second group started a foster home for four younger children. A group of women who belonged to the same Presbyterian Church in Arlington, VA, sponsored a foster home near where they lived.

ENVISIONING ALTERNATIVES TO
JUNIOR VILLAGE

Following an orientation course that grew out of the first sessions, members of the First Methodist Church of Hyattsville, MD, formed a group. They chose a dual mission: setting up a foster home for five children and designing a plan for a large network of foster homes, where salaried foster parents would be partners in a team with social workers and volunteers. Before designing the alternative system, they wrote to a dozen U.S. cities, asking about their child welfare system and how it had changed. Many cities described how social service professionals themselves had led the struggle to close custodial institutions and replace them with community-based alternatives.

The information gathered from other cities spurred the FLOC "Hyattsville Mission Group" to think out an alternative foster care system for DC. The group prepared a printed document, "Better Care at Less Cost for Washington's Homeless Children," and took it to the DPW Director. The director was obviously impressed that a volunteer community group would address what she considered the public agency's problem, but she essentially ignored the proposal.

Next FLOC took the "Better Care at Less Cost" report to the House and Senate Committees that handled District of Columbia legislation and appropriated the DC budget. Two friendly committee chairmen, Congressman William Natcher of Kentucky and Senator William Proxmire of Wisconsin, became keenly interested in the work of FLOC and invited us to present our alternative proposal at the annual budget hearings for DPW. (Mr. Natcher happened to be a friend of my father, who had encouraged him to run for Congress years before.) FLOC was commended for its plan, and DPW was instructed to develop an alternative to Junior Village within 30 days.

In some ways this venture in Congress was a charade, because Congressional staff didn't have the time or the knowledge to follow up on the directive. But one thing did result: FLOC gained DPW's attention as a community group to be taken seriously. Moreover, DPW could not completely ignore what FLOC was saying because they would be accountable to the committee a year hence at budget time.

CHANGE FROM WITHIN THE SYSTEM

At the same time as first the Coalition of Conscience and then FLOC pressed from the outside for systemic change, initiatives for change also came from within the bureaucracy.

Albert Russo, deputy director of DPW, was a consummate bureaucrat. He knew how to avoid alienating both people below him who could implement new ideas and people above him who authorized and funded the ideas. He treated people on the outside with consistent courtesy, while revealing little of his plans. Russo was silently pleased at the enthusiasm being generated for welfare reform and for closing Junior Village. He could not, however, openly oppose Senator Byrd, who at that time controlled District of Columbia fiscal decision making.

When Russo had been appointed deputy director, he had moved to Washington and lived for several months in a government apartment at Junior Village. During the purge of the welfare rolls he watched the population increase almost daily. Years later he told me he had nightmares about a fire breaking out and killing hundreds of children. He had repeatedly emphasized to his superior the danger of Junior Village becoming a public disaster.

As the community drumbeat for change intensified and the Economic Opportunity Act of 1965 appropriated money, Russo outlined a program designed to prevent separation of families. He implemented new emergency financial aid, emergency shelter, and job training programs. These new programs were the major factor in the reduction of the population at Junior Village from 900 to 600 in one year. These programs helped roll away the stone over the lives of Junior Village children.

FLOC EXPANDS

As FLOC and other agencies recruited foster parents, opened homes, found housing for families, and put pressure on the system from the outside, the population at Junior Village began to fall. We began to believe that it might be possible to supplant the institution altogether. Through the fall, winter, and spring orientation courses, 13 mission groups were formed. Several groups came from specific churches—

Arlington Unitarian, Redeemer Lutheran of McLean, a Lay Franciscan Catholic fellowship in the Virginia suburbs, Shiloh Baptist church in downtown Washington, New York Avenue Presbyterian church, a suburban Presbyterian church, and a fellowship of African American women. Other groups were ecumenical. Even some of the unchurched found the combination of small group nurture and social action surprisingly invigorating.

Ten of these mission groups focused on creating foster homes where a married couple or a pair of women would care for four to five able children or two handicapped children.

This plan generated over 100 new foster placements in four years. There were several problems, however: divided allegiances and inconsistent social services, which led eventually to FLOC's transition from a mostly volunteer organization to a service-providing organization run by professionals. FLOC foster parents, better educated than most foster parents at the time, demanded superior educational and health care services for their children. DPW was unable to satisfy these demands, and so FLOC began to develop a professional staff to provide services the foster children needed.

Support services were substantially improved, but something else was lost. Foster parents gradually ceased to be prime movers in FLOC, and the volunteer support system faded away as professionals took over. For these staff members and foster parents, the focus shifted from participation in a movement to get children out of Junior Village to the day to day struggle to raise foster children with very special needs. For myself and other volunteers, the focus continued to be on changing the system itself.

ADVOCACY AND EDUCATION

While expending enormous effort to develop foster homes, FLOC expanded its initial advocacy work. A prominent FLOC group was the "Systems Change Task Force," first convened by Dr. Ann Maney, a sociologist at the National Institute of Mental Health. This four-month community seminar explored a systems approach to closing and replacing Junior Village. Members of FLOC and other community organizations, DPW social workers, and university and hospital professionals responded to her invitation to participate. Local officials and national experts were invited to discuss both the existing child welfare system and proposals for a better system.

In the seminar, we imaged the DC child welfare system as a funnel. Children were flowing into this funnel at the rate of over 100 per month. The causes were multiple and complex: lack of housing, lack of income, and lack of support structures for the family, mental illness, acute physical illness, incarceration, or immaturity of the parent. (This was prior to the advent of crack cocaine several years later.)

The task force framed several questions. First, how can this community substantially reduce the number of children entering the system? How can it better support families to stay together? How can it widen the exits to the system and reduce the time children stay in the system? How can the community ensure good care for children in the system? What is the structure of the current system and the philosophy on which it is based?

As we worked with these questions, we decided to approach the DC City Council with our ideas for change. We were listened to politely, but nothing changed, except our understanding of the politics of the situation.

PUBLIC OUTCRY FOR
CLOSING JUNIOR VILLAGE

A few weeks after making the rounds of City Council members to no effect, a meeting occurred, which would in fact lead directly to the closing of Junior Village. Finally, it was time. In the Greek language there are two words for time: chronos, meaning linear time, and kairos, meaning special time. Things happen in kairos time that chronos time has prepared for. It was kairos time for the children of Junior Village.

Martin Fields was an African American social worker at Junior Village. In his eyes, Junior Village carried out nothing less than the genocide of black children. He was firmly convinced that the institution would not be allowed to exist if the majority of the children were white instead of black. Fields saw Junior Village as a warehouse where children from 6 months of age to 18 were at best neglected and at worst physically and emotionally abused.

The institution was unable to provide emotional nurturance to children already traumatized by separation from parents, and in fact, did additional harm. He reported incidents of rape, physical abuse, and staff members involving children in organized theft in the neighborhood. For three years Fields wrote a stream of memos documenting and protesting the abuse and neglect. The memos were ignored, except for polite routine acknowledgments. Meanwhile, he kept copies of everything sent and received.

Fields initiated a meeting with me, and I took him to J.W. Anderson, a friend on the editorial staff of *The Washington Post* who had written numerous articles about Junior Village. When Anderson saw the notebook he slapped it and said, "This is the kind of documentation we have been waiting for!"

Aaron Latham, a young reporter, was assigned to the story, and editors decided to run a four-part series on Junior Village. The first three articles detailed inferior care and specific incidents of abuse of children. The fourth focused on alternatives, using the FLOC Foster Home Program as an example of a better approach.

The coverage provoked heated community reaction and volumes of mail. The city administration was very defensive. The mayor transferred the administrator of Junior Village, but this, of course, was beside the point. Andy Jacobs, Congressman from Indiana, arranged a press conference for me, and then a series of public hearings. The hearings attracted such attention that they were carried live over public radio, and the newspapers gave them prominent coverage. Aaron Latham was relentless in his reporting, and later won a national award for his coverage.

The newly established City Council of the District of Columbia, not to be outdone by the Congress, called hearings of its own. This gave the opportunity for broader testimony, and kept the issue prominent in the press. FLOC laid out a comprehensive set of alternatives to Junior Village, drawing on its year-long study in Dr. Maney's seminar.

The Urban League, the Child Welfare League of America, and scores of community groups and private agencies called for the replacement of Junior Village with community-based alternatives. City Councilman Stanley Anderson presented the plan to the City Council, and it was adopted by the Council with one dissenting vote. Mayor Walter Washington, however, for political reasons, refused to either sign or veto the Council plan, but appointed his own "blue ribbon" panel of national experts to study the problem and recommend a solution. Against this diversionary strategy, Councilman Stanley Anderson introduced a resolution ordering the closing of Junior Village in two years.

DPW and the Mayor did not oppose the City Council mandate. They accepted the timetable—no children under six in the institution by the end of 12 months, no children older than six placed in the institution after 18 months, and the closing of the facility within 24 months. To accomplish this, DPW expanded its contracting for foster homes and group homes with private agencies, including FLOC. In a few instances it simply transferred handicapped children to other city-run institutions. Unfortunately, public planners concentrated on expanding foster care and neglected the crucial family preservation services. In short, the victory was partial. Much work remained to be done to open wide the tomb of Washington, DC's abused and neglected children. Nonetheless, a rock had been rolled away and the system pointed in a new direction.

REFLECTIONS ON SOCIAL CHANGE

What brought about the closing of Junior Village? How did a group of ordinary people roll this stone away, in a large and complex city in the last part of the 20th century in the United States?

The most salient point is this: no single action or person made the difference. It was a matter of the convergence of energies: persistence, people holding a vision, people continuing when they were tired, publicity, confrontation, time, luck, knowledge and planning, insiders and outsiders—all coming together in what can be called kairos time.

VISION

Gordon Cosby shared a tangible vision of a home for every child. This was specific enough to be compelling and large enough to stretch people's hearts. And he invented the vision through solitary reflection and participation in a larger social movement. He listened for what the events of his time were saying. Then he deliberately opened his mind and heart to see an alternative vision and to hear the word calling him to action.

Cosby came to the vision by holding the ways this institution was violating deep community values alongside images of those values being realized—the suffering of children whose right to a family was violated vis a vis images of community support for families in crisis. The contradiction brought Cosby to a point of outrage. Then he had to live with the outrage long enough to get past being controlled by his emotions and see concrete steps to take.

It was clear. It was simple. The vision of a home for every child provided both momentum for the journey and boundaries for the variety of energies offered, like the banks of a fast-flowing river.

SHARING THE VISION

Cosby and others brought the possible to consciousness: a vision of children raised with compassion in families whose basic needs were met. That was compelling. It caused people's hearts to beat faster. And it helped them see the lack of vision in Junior Village.

People responded to the vision because it was spoken clearly, often, and through a variety of forms. A volunteer-led after school art class for elementary age children at Junior Village produced an expressive drawing that was made into a Christmas card. Volunteers put words expressing the vision to old music, such as the Battle Hymn of the Republic, to add spirit and contemporaneity to FLOC meetings. Communication through the Sunday afternoon briefing sessions, volunteers calling all the churches in the Yellow Pages, the mission groups, the Bible study, the Maney seminar, a newsletter blew on the flame. Also, people responded because the vision called out the best in them—their highest values, their most compassionate and altruistic impulses.

LEADERSHIP

Another key to success was strong shared leadership and a continuity of leadership. Power was shared. Leadership was seen as something one invested in for a while, then passed on to someone else.

Organization by small groups, each with its own clear vision and task, meant that the groups could meet many of the personal and interpersonal needs of the activists and thus free energy for constructive action. Many projects go awry because the unmet needs of the actors for recognition, inclusion, and affection compete for attention with accomplishing the task. Undernourished people, paid or unpaid, make competitive rather than collaborative activists. An explicit philosophy of high trust and low control meant that volunteers, as well as paid staff members, were given significant responsibility and the authority to act.

Small groups worked together with leaders willing to be responsible. And both worked well with the help of a mentor.

MENTORING

Ann Maney's mentoring made it possible for a minister like me; a scientist like Jim Ritter, the first President of FLOC; and other people with no direct training in social work, child welfare, or the changing of social systems to learn as we went along. Without being anyone's supervisor, Ann guided us with her extensive knowledge and encouraging spirit. She also played a major role in helping Congressman Andy Jacobs' staff set up the crucial public hearings and invite witnesses. Others played a similar mentoring/coaching role in other areas of expertise, from counseling to financial management and fund raising.

A SPIRITUAL BASE

Woven into the small groups and the larger structure of FLOC was a truly ecumenical, noncoercive spiritual dimension that kept us going. We began to be ecumenical when we called every religious community in the phone book, and we never lost that inclusive spirit. We had no belief system that each person had to adopt, though many of us were open about our conviction that God was calling us to this work, and that the work of justice is the work of spiritual people.

Our religion was not allowed to be abstracted from the realities of human suffering in the 20th century. It called for a heavy commitment of individuals on behalf of the poor, the city, the oppressed. The call to social justice is an essential part of spiritual formation, and cannot be isolated for one on the journey toward wholeness.

There was no ax to grind theologically, no denomination to please. There was need. There was a call. There were the various gifts that individuals brought to the call of the group. It was a noncoercive, non-guilt-producing message. And people who hadn't gone to church in years found the combination of spirituality, small group life, and social change work very appealing.

HOMEWORK

FLOC was well informed, not just well meaning. We had done our homework, and we did it consistently, over and over. The Hyattsville Mission Group is a good example. FLOC made sure that every time we were called on to present our case—in newspaper articles, in hearings, in press conferences—we had thoroughly researched our position and our recommendations.

Through Dr. Maney's seminar, we educated ourselves, learning about the system and how it worked and how to get things done.

We learned that much of the process was political. We learned that change of the magnitude of closing Junior Village seldom happens without becoming a political issue and involving the political process.

LEARNING HOW THE SYSTEM WORKS

FLOC got to know and learned to work with people in power. We used all the political contacts we had, then cultivated other politicians who became invaluable allies.

With Albert Russo we learned about the role of a system "insider." Too often we on the outside see bureaucracies as closed, relatively frozen monoliths instead of organisms that incorporate competing viewpoints and centers of power. The closing of Junior Village could not have occurred without the fermentation of fresh ideas on the inside and a two-way flow of information. Even though Russo appeared to be stonewalling the community effort to close Junior Village, he cajoled resistant forces on the inside to implement new programs.

Our relationships with bureaucrats and city council members who were friendly to us were similar to the one we cultivated with Russo.

We learned that the press could help us get the word out, by capitalizing on a story that had so much human interest people couldn't help responding. We used our contacts in the local papers to help break the story and bring pressure to bear on public officials.

RELATIONSHIPS BETWEEN PERSONS

We learned about the importance of all kinds of relationships, from our relationship with Albert Russo and the City Council to the relationships of FLOC volunteers to families. We didn't just throw money or even time and energy at the problem. We got involved, and we taught the people who joined us to get involved. We learned that the transforming power of relationships would carry people a long way. Often relating was the most difficult part, but it remained a central value.

TIMING

We learned to pay attention to what was happening, and to use what we saw happening to move toward our vision. We learned to put in our time, to be persistent, and to wait for the kairos moment to be given. When Junior Village social worker Martin Fields stepped forward so courageously to tell his story, we worked with this opportunity for public education, while recognizing the potential cost to Martin and to ourselves. We learned to watch for opportunities like this, for the openings, for the gifts.

It was a grace-filled experience. It was watching for God at work in the whole enterprise, seeing that all our hard work and knowledge wouldn't do a thing unless the time was right.

One stone was rolled away. Of course there are other stones, other tombs. But we succeeded, by collaborative action, over a period of years, in freeing some children and some families to live more fully.

We were the community of people standing around the sealed tomb. We were commanded, by the events of our time as well as by our inner voices and by our perception of a God who leads, to act. Commanded to act, we had our doubts; but we did it. We moved this stone, opened this grave. Such actions set the stage for the next act, the command: "Lazarus, come forth!"

Chapter Seven

POOR AND NON-POOR AS PARTNERS

It happened! The stone was moved. The tomb of Lazarus was opened. Institutionalized children at Junior Village were returned home or placed in home-like settings. New possibilities were at hand. But this is only the beginning of the process of liberation for the children, and in the Biblical story. It is not the end, not even the climax.

Act II is Jesus' part. He is the healer, the catalyst. He calls loudly into the tomb, "Lazarus, come forth!"

What in the world can he expect? This is absurd. Unbelievable. There's no one in there who can hear. The friends stand amazed.

He calls again.

Suddenly a stirring and a shifting. What is this?

The dead man has heard his name called. He has awakened at the sound of it, and he is coming out! What shape will he be in? What can we expect from one dead for four days?

THE CALLING OF THE NAME

People often ask what ever happened to the Civil Rights Movement. Why were most of the black poor left behind in economic misery, not to mention the white poor? What difference did the Civil Rights Movement make?

It made a profound difference. There is no doubt about it. The stone of segregation—legal segregation anyway—was rolled away. A host of courageous, determined, creative people, blacks and whites in partnership with one another and the God of history, pushed against a huge stone and it moved.

Out of that opened tomb poured millions of people who had been ready for years, waiting for the opportunity to enter restaurants, swimming pools, neighborhoods, schools, jobs, and professions from which they had been excluded. The particular African American people who benefited from the overturning of legal segregation, however, were largely middle class. They were equipped to compete in white institutions. Most came from strong families, had been good students in the black school system, and were capable of learning and growing at the same rate as their white peers once they were given the chance.

Sadly, the people at the bottom of society were barely affected by the successes of the Civil Rights Movement. Those who were deepest in the cave of poverty did not hear their names called. Why was this?

LEARNED HELPLESSNESS

Recently I asked Lionel Haman, an experienced counselor in FLOC's therapeutic group home for adolescent boys, to name the toughest single problem he faced in getting the young people ready for independent living. Without hesitation he said, "Overcoming learned helplessness."

Children can learn to be helpless just as they can learn to be resourceful. The difference generally depends on the pattern of interaction between the child and the parent(s). In a strong family, children are given to generously and expected to give back in proportion to their age and maturity. Nobody beyond infancy gets a free ride. There just isn't enough energy to do all that needs doing for the family to get along well unless everyone pitches in. Parents with healthy self-respect as well as a strong bond with their children see the family as a joint enterprise. Close family living is a giving-receiving proposition punctuated by perpetual negotiation. This multidimensional, ever-expanding give and take prepares the young for the larger world.

Some children never experience this kind of inclusion, with the consequence that they withhold themselves emotionally from adults and in many cases also from their peers.

Deprived children, consequently, whether rich or poor, are often notoriously manipulative. Mistrusting that they can get what they want from adults by an open request or negotiation, they get it by appealing to adult guilt while investing little of themselves. Adults who work with these children face the constant suction of giving—attention, material goods, privileges—without receiving—cooperation or valuing of the gifts. Many children who are trying to break away from adult dominance and become their own persons act like this sometimes, but severely deprived youths manipulate by appearing helpless much of the time. The adult usually responds by offering bribes to keep the child in line. This makes the manipulation reciprocal. As the pattern builds both the child and the adult come to view the other with anger and contempt. The relationship becomes silent hostility at best and outright abuse at worst.

To an alarming extent this negative adult-child pattern also describes the interaction between the persistently poor and the innumerable institutions designed to serve them. Manipulation runs both ways, as do anger and contempt. When the poor go to social service offices, health clinics, or employment offices, they expect to be perceived as objects, because that is what they have known. As objects, they perceive themselves as powerless, except for their power to manipulate, working from a stance of learned helplessness. They select what information they will share and withhold the rest. A helper who works out of a mutual respect, empowerment paradigm is up against these deeply entrenched perceptions, which are extremely hard to overcome.

When the poor sense genuine caring and respect from a worker or volunteer, they are both attracted and suspicious. For anything new to happen, the poor have to give permission for the helper to get behind their protective walls. The decision rests with them. Some are content with the game of learned helplessness, of pushing buttons so that the helper will make their life easier without introducing the threat of change. Others are ready to come forth at the call of their name. They can respond to an empowering partnership, in which the helper offers information, tools, support, recognition of their worth, and love for them as subjects.

There is more to liberation and empowerment than just agreeing to be helped. Paulo Freire, a Brazilian educator known around the world for his pioneering work teaching illiterate peasants to read in a few weeks, says that the only way the plight of the oppressed ever changes is by their becoming active in their own liberation.

Although his thinking and educational methodology were worked out in a Third World setting, I believe Freire addresses what many consider the hopeless plight of the persistently poor in this country. He does not see poverty as either necessary or inevitable in either the developed or underdeveloped worlds. He believes that real, sustainable change must involve a dynamic, dual process that he calls praxis. It is impossible to change the situation of the poor from the outside alone. That is the approach of traditional charity. That is band-aid methodology. In reality it is a subtle form of domestication, siphoning off the frustration and rage of trapped people. It holds the powerless in place and reinforces their powerlessness. It is not a process that empowers people to rise up to their full stature. It treats the poor like children and rewards the most compliant, the cleverest, or even the most demanding children.

PRAXIS

Praxis is a process of change involving both poor and non-poor, and because it involves both, it requires a fundamental shift in perception. A key concept is the difference between seeing one's self as object or seeing one's self as subject; and between seeing other people as subjects and seeing them as objects. Objects are known and acted upon; subjects, in contrast, both know and act. Praxis is about the awakening of social groups and individuals who are treated as objects to the experience of themselves as subjects. For the non-poor, praxis entails a shift in both self-perception and perception of the poor; the shift from seeing poor people as objects of charity, pity, and coercion to seeing them as persons who, like ourselves, are gifted, intelligent, and unique.

Freire's contention is that every human being, no matter how unlettered or how deeply submerged in the culture of silence, can engage in a genuine encounter with others. Provided with the proper tools, she can gradually perceive her personal and social reality (and the contradictions in it) and deal intelligently with that reality. But first the tools must be provided.

Freire believes strongly in the power that comes with the ability to use language. An educated person can use words to communicate experience and dialogue with others. In working in villages in northeast Brazil, where few adults could read, Freire and his colleagues started by simply listening to ordinary village conversation. They listened particularly for what Freire calls "generative themes," that is, issues of special significance to village life which, if brought to consciousness, would release energy for action. In one village, for example, water was a generative theme. In that village there was only one source of water, a single well. Water had to be carried for cooking, washing, watering gardens. The daily transport of water, largely by hand, consumed a major portion of every family's energy.

This is the way it had always been. During periods of drought, conversation reflected the fatalism of village consciousness: "It is the will of God." Theirs was a closed universe, and lacking the ability to read, they could not expose themselves to alternative universes. Freire calls this a "culture of silence." His objective was to empower these illiterate people by breaking open their closed universe. He not only gave them the tools of reading and writing, but also taught them to apply the tool of language to describe their predicament, to question why it was so, and to engage in a discussion about what they might do to change it.

To invite discussion, the educators drew pictures of the village well with people coming and going away carrying water. As the discussion went on, they would spell out in large letters the key words the villagers were using and point out nouns like water and well in the drawings. They introduced vocabulary after it had surfaced in the discussion. In that way it dawned on the people that there was nothing wrong with their ability to think. What they needed were tools to project their thinking visually to others and to preserve their ideas.

The energy of the learners expanded as they acquired additional words to carry the meanings they were conveying to each other. As their energy grew, their attention expanded to problem solving. Someone reported that a nearby village had built a system to move water from a spring through pipes to spigots scattered around the village. What caused that to happen? The learners pushed through the boundaries of their closed universe, their culture of silence. They began to probe cause and effect.

Someone proposed that they appoint a delegation to go to that village and investigate. They went and reported back. Then a delegation was sent to the provincial capital to request assistance with what they now defined as their water problem. All the time outside educators fed in through picture and discussion the visual representations of the words the villagers were using in their animated conversation. A change of consciousness was taking place. Energy replaced apathy. Through this praxis of engaging together in probing village reality and questioning that reality, the villagers experienced themselves as active subjects rather than passive objects.

EMPOWERMENT

The impact upon the participants was dramatic. Freire reports that again and again, after even a few classes, peasants would describe themselves in language filled with excitement. "I now realize I am a man, an educated man." "We were blind, now our eyes have been opened." "Before this, words meant nothing to me; now they speak to me and I can make them speak." "Now we will no longer be a dead weight on the cooperative farm."[1]

Freire's thinking took shape in a Third World country, among people with no previous access to education. Except for a few wealthy landowners and their managers, everyone in those rural communities was poor. There was no middle class per se. The contrasts were sharp and clear. Because the poor were so visible and in the majority, there was great potential for group solidarity once they became active in shaping their future.

In contrast, poverty in the United States is much more diffuse, and oppression much more subtle. Those who see themselves and are seen by social institutions (school, church, courts) as the persistently poor are a distinct minority. When visible they stand out with a degree of powerlessness that invites paternalism or disrespect. Moreover, while concentrated to some extent in poor neighborhoods and rural enclaves, the persistently poor in this country are also highly transient. Many lack fixed addresses. They live temporarily with friends, with relatives, in public shelters, in cars, or on the streets. They do not stay long enough or dare to become visible enough to be recognized as neighbors. Some of the poor who have fixed addresses are too proud to admit their suffering and need. They get by with very little heat in the winter and subsist on diets that are injurious to themselves and their children.

Given the relatively low social visibility of poverty in the United States, how do we make use of Freire's keen insight into the praxis of liberation? How do we in Jesus' stead say to our entombed countrymen, women, and children, "Come forth out of that tomb!"? What does Lazarus' "Yes" sound like in the context of persistent poverty today?

Freire's teaching methodology, like his philosophy, is built on the premise that the coming forth of the poor out of the tomb requires learning, incorporating the learning into action, and learning from the action, which leads to further action. The scale and complexity of the action must fit the initial and growing capacity of the particular group, family, or individual. Freire's idea of liberating praxis is to start small and simple, with the graspable issues at hand.

In some ways this is a gradualist approach; however, in the mental, spiritual, and psychological realms it is revolutionary. It is the self building the self, the group building the group. The helper provides tools so the entrapped person can make her way through the impasse step by step. In this country we have got to understand that the best helpers, the best allies of the poor, are those who are most perceptive and appreciative of the strengths of the poor, both individually and collectively. The guiding word is empowerment.

THE RESPONSE OF LAZARUS: ROCK CLIMBING

I gained some important insights about my own empowerment through a rock climbing experience on the Outward Bound course I mentioned earlier.

In teaching us to climb a perpendicular rock face, the instructor told us, "The first thing you have to get into your heads is to take what the rock gives you." When you first look at a difficult climb, you cannot see how you can get up the cliff. But then, as you look more carefully, you see a tiny foothold here, a crevice for your fingers there, then a slight depression. If you put one foot here, you can put your fingers there, and the other foot there. You can't see how to get to the top from where you are, but you can see how you might get to the next level. You take what the rock gives you. Each time you shift your weight from the lower to the higher foot, you experience the danger of falling. You are hooked up to a safety harness, but you have to actively trust both that equipment and the person at the top holding it.

Midway up the cliff I encountered an area so smooth that the rock gave me nothing. I was on a tiny ledge, eight inches wide and narrowing to nothing. Whatever trail there was had ended. It seemed impossible to work my way back down. Anticipating this impasse, the instructor threw down a knotted rope from the top. It hung five feet out of my reach.

I yelled to the instructor, "Come on now, Jerry, move it over here."

"Go for it!" he called down.

I said, "It's too far."

He said, "You can make it. This is about trust, Fred."

I thought, "Yeah, trust! Do I trust you? Do I trust that rope?"

Then the thought hit me, "Do I trust me?"

I stood transfixed for what seemed like minutes, weighing my options, trembling with fear. I looked down at the jagged rocks and water 100 feet below. I decided to go for it. Taking a deep breath and gathering all my strength, I leaped for the dangling rope, and somehow I caught it. I used it to pull myself up the smooth rock to the top.

When I got there, I raised my arms, gave a resounding Tarzan yell, and jumped up and down. The feeling in my 53-year-old body lingered for several days and comes back even now as I remember the experience. I had gone beyond my self-imposed limits. I had gone through my fear. I had taken a leap of faith. I marveled at my own courage. I saw myself then as a person who was willing to risk, and that sense of myself will never be erased.

I came home thinking that I want this experience for the youth and parents of FLOC, for my fellow staff people, for all people. Outward Bound set the stage. The instructors and my companions cheered me on; but it was I who took the leap, who experienced the empowerment, who now has that wonderful, self-affirming memory.

This experience may seem remote from any application to the poor, most of whom lack the physical strength for rock climbing or the money for an Outward Bound course. But I see it as another metaphor for coming out of the tomb. It is a story about claiming one's own power, risking exposure to the sunlight after long conditioning to the closed universe of a tomb.

A realistic praxis must embody such an empowering experience on the part of the poor. The praxis may start from either side, but there will be risk-taking on both sides, and in that risk-taking new power emerges. The formerly powerless claim for themselves what they did not previously think possible.

Here are two examples of a praxis leading to change, one of a neighborhood and the other of an individual.

KENILWORTH-PARKSIDE

Several years ago, two youths in a rundown, crime ridden public housing project in northeast Washington sought out the only adult they knew who had a college education. They asked her to help them go to college. This woman, Kimi Gray, had moved into the Kenilworth-Parkside project at the age of 22, a divorced mother of four children. At the time she was living on public assistance and public housing was the only kind she could afford. After she got a job with the city recreation department, she gradually worked her way through college.

When these youths asked her help she did some investigating and found that only two children raised in that project had ever gone to college. With the two as her partners, she set up a study hall, and invited other young people. They put together a program with the nearby schools to ensure that anyone who wanted to could take college preparatory classes. She raised money to take young people to visit colleges, and located scholarship funds. Students began to go away to college as well as attend local colleges.

At that time Kenilworth-Parkside was under private management, and the landlord often ignored requests for repairs. Kimi and other residents discussed what they could do to change their situation. It was a mayoral election year, so they invited mayoral candidates to visit the project. They proposed that the management contract be transferred to the tenants. Marion Barry, the incumbent, promised to effect that change if reelected. The project turned out a good vote and Barry delivered on his promise. The tenant organization began collecting rents and maintaining the buildings. When they found residents with particular skills the project needed, such as installing storm windows, they hired them. Rental income increased substantially and money began to circulate within the project community. For the first time the project showed a profit.

Tenants persuaded the city to let them use the profit to set up a free day care center for mothers who worked or were in job training. With tenant organization encouragement, several small businesses, including a barber shop, a beauty shop, and a boutique, were started, and over 100 jobs were created.

The "College, Here We Come" program has now sent over 600 people to college. The percentage of families on welfare has dropped from 80% to 20%. The crime rate has dropped below that of the middle class housing development across the street. And, in the words of Kimi Gray, "The men started coming back." Unemployed fathers had left so their families could get public assistance, and sons, brothers, and fathers had given up fitting into mainstream society. The ratio of adult males to females and fathers to sons increased.

Here is an example of a genuine rollback of poverty through a praxis of change. Kimi Gray, like Moses, went outside the community to get an education and then used both her acquired skills and her native gifts to lead her people toward freedom. Power was not conferred from the outside; power was claimed from the inside, one step at a time. Kimi Gray recognized and responded to a need, and she used her organizing skills to pull people together for mutual empowerment.

There was a dialectic between the organized power of this poor community and the city power structure, under widespread criticism for the deteriorated, dangerous state of public housing. The two parties had something to offer each other. The people in Kenilworth-Parkside ceased to be "objects" to the city government. The city, faced with a steady hemorrhage of public tax moneys, came to realize that here was a potential ally rather than a burden. City officials saw that they were dealing with intelligent people who knew what they wanted. City officials also knew the power of the ballot box. This is how the destructive inequity of power begins to shift: those with power understand that it is in their self-interest to negotiate with those they previously saw as powerless, once the latter start exerting the power of the ballot.

The Kenilworth-Parkside story is a modern day, First World version of the calling of Lazarus from the tomb. In this case, Lazarus heard the call, and used the life force given him to walk out of the tomb.

ADRIENNE GOODE

An example of praxis at the individual and family level is the story of a former FLOC staff member, Adrienne Goode. Adrienne grew up in poverty in a female-headed household in Detroit, as did her mother before her. She had forebears who were property owners in Mississippi, but somewhere along the line the family had lost the land.

As a teenager Adrienne had been selected by a federally funded Upward Bound program, whose goal was to prepare poor minority students for college and help them get scholarships. After the thrill of being selected, Adrienne began to experience severe inner conflict about succeeding. She was confident she could handle the college level work, for she had always been a bright student. But she felt guilty about having an opportunity not afforded her sister and her mother, who supported the three of them as a domestic worker. The mother herself had very mixed feelings about her daughter's opportunity. She was afraid she would lose her daughter, afraid that if Adrienne finished college she would leave her family and neighborhood behind. She might even look down on them. Adrienne knew her mother's fear, and she also feared being shut out of the family. Upward Bound had a policy of requiring its students to attend a college at least 200 miles from home, in order to diminish negative family influence. Adrienne wondered, "Do I have to choose between a different future for myself and my bond with my family?"

Finally, she risked the separation. She took the leap of faith. She went for the rope that offered a way up the rock wall. With the strong support of the federal program she went off to college, finished, and then went on to earn a master's degree. But she did not reject her family, nor, as it turned out, did they withdraw from her. Instead, her younger sister followed in her footsteps and finished college, and her mother, in her forties, started night school, trained as a practical nurse, and launched a career.

Breaking out of persistent poverty is far more complex than helping bright students develop their potential. Poverty is both economic and spiritual in nature. Calling people out of it involves money, lots of it, but also far more than money. It requires a joint effort, a joining with, a mutually respecting praxis.

It requires a Jesus to call the name of Lazarus, his friend, just as it requires Lazarus to use the energies and capacities awakened by the calling of his name. And it sets the stage for the further unbinding that the friends of Lazarus are asked to do for him.

Chapter Eight

STORIES OF EMPOWERMENT

When Lazarus emerged from the opened tomb he was alive, but so bound by the layers of grave wrappings that he could barely walk. Jesus saw his condition and gave another charge to the community: "Unbind him, let him go."

The work wasn't done yet! For this man to be free he needed further help. The cloth binding his legs, trunk, arms, and head to preserve the body from disintegration had to be removed. He had to be fully freed. Jesus would settle for nothing less. So he called the community into action again. Layer by layer the people unwrapped the body of their neighbor, unwinding and peeling back the layers of fabric. Lazarus moved and turned as they directed him, feeling the blood rush into constricted limbs, feeling the cool air on his skin once again.

Each of the actions in the Lazarus story is concrete: 1) the rolling away of a stone, 2) the victim stepping out of the tomb, 3) the unwrapping of the grave cloths from the victim. Any praxis of liberation must be equally concrete.

FOSTER CHILDREN

Here are some examples of concrete acts of unbinding foster children. As FLOC became intimately involved with fostering children and reuniting birth families, we learned how much unbinding work there was to be done. While Junior Village was in existence, the children there were highly visible to the city as a collective group, but invisible as individuals. They traveled to public school in a school bus marked Junior Village, and as a group they presented so many problems they were tagged "Junior Village children." Junior Village was also highly visible as a favorite target for community charity. Literally hundreds of organizations chose Junior Village as their annual project for "doing good."

Once the children were reunited with their birth parents or put in foster homes, they shed this collective identity and became visible as individuals.

HEALTH CARE

Long neglected health and dental problems were readily apparent in many foster and institutionalized children. And the discrimination against these children by the public system mandated to serve them was apparent too. Sandy Eastep, a foster parent and member of a FLOC mission group, was also a trained nurse. One day she took her four-year old foster child for his annual physical. Over the objection of the clinic nurse, she insisted upon remaining with him as he received his physical. When the doctor stopped after a cursory examination she protested. He replied matter of factly, "Well, lady, if you want a full examination, you can see me in my private practice. They don't pay me to do that at this clinic."

Sandy hit the ceiling. She took her story back to her mission group. When she compared stories with other foster parents, she found strong dissatisfaction with health services. In time, FLOC hired her as a part-time health advocate, coaching FLOC foster parents to expect quality health care for their children, and addressing health issues with city administrators.

EDUCATION

Many of the foster children were educationally handicapped. Deprivation, emotional problems, and learning disabilities were some of the causes. One 12-year-old boy was such a problem that the principal had him sent home every day at noon, after only a half day of school.

Soon FLOC hired an educational specialist to monitor the progress of all the children in our family foster homes. Valli Matthews, with a master's degree in special education, found many services available in the public schools, but she also noticed a lack of documentation of children's needs. It took careful, painstaking negotiating with the system to obtain needed services.

Grace Dickerson, a former teacher on the staff of the Hope and a Home program, began an educational advocacy project for children living with their birth families. Poor children with their birth families do not have the same access to the services available as children in the foster care system. Once they return to their birth families their needs are entirely the parent's responsibility. Moreover, inner city schools have so many children with special needs that a child has to act out in dramatic ways before s/he can get special help. Passive children who fall two and three grade levels behind in reading and math are routinely overlooked. Many poor parents are perceptive enough to recognize their child has a learning problem, but getting professional attention requires more knowledge, skill, and persistence than they may have. Grace worked with several families in the FLOC Hope and a Home program, and reported that each case was like climbing a mountain. She found many resources for children with educational disabilities, even free legal help, but getting and maintaining the services required intensive child-by-child advocacy.

Grace now teaches parents their rights, runs a tutoring program, trains experienced parents to work with less experienced, and builds linkages with the system. The prevailing assumption of the system is that it is impossible to actually educate every child, given the high level of need. This is nothing more than triage. Since special placements cost from $5,000 to $50,000 per year, only a small percentage can be given that attention. Current law, however, says otherwise: every child is entitled to an education appropriate to her needs, and the public system must provide it or place the child in a private program and pay the cost.

Recent research indicates that you can tell by behavior in third-grade children who is likely to drop out before finishing high school. The problems these children manifest, if flagged early and addressed, can be diminished, if not overcome altogether.

This is an unbinding issue. It is very concrete. We can do something about it. A single church or group of churches can decide to press the matter until third-grade children at risk in a particular neighborhood elementary school are identified and helped. This is a very specific, very do-able action.

As the examples of health and educational advocacy illustrate, translating the call of Jesus to unbind poor children and their parents requires doing battle with the status quo. It requires dealing with public systems in support of an entire class of persons while continuing the work of unbinding individuals.

THERAPEUTIC GROUP HOMES

Another example of concrete acts of unbinding is FLOC's therapeutic group home for 10 adolescent males. Phil Davis, the group home director, is a highly skilled youth worker with an exceptional knack for getting kids who don't trust anyone to open up. Recently he shared with me his philosophy of child care. "What I am trying to do," he said, "is establish a climate of winning. We are taking on kids who expect to lose. They expect others to let them down, so they hide their fears behind a macho exterior. One thing I do is hold a 15-minute group meeting every morning before they leave for school. I say, 'What we are about today is winning! Let's talk about how we are going to do that.'"

Before I got to know Phil this would have struck me as phony. But I knew the case histories of the 10 African American street kids in that home. Seeing their respect for Phil, also African American, I had to take another look.

These are kids whose fathers died, went to prison, or left the family when they were small. Few of them have had a close, continuing relationship with an adult male. No one has been there to help them develop confidence as men. What they have learned about being men they have picked up mostly in the streets.

These young men want to be Somebody. They want respect.

Their behavior, however, suggests the opposite. They have been poor achievers in school. They give up easily when they meet frustration. They have poor control over their impulses, and when they're angry they quickly turn to inflicting pain on whomever is nearby, adults or peers, acquaintances or strangers. Their lives are a perpetual con game, a power struggle with adult authority figures. They love to test their skill in "getting over," that is, making fools of others, particularly adults. They have no idea that any adult, especially a male, could be deeply interested in them and strong and loving enough to stop their games of "getting over."

They have developed profound psychological defenses against letting adults get close. Yet within their protected psychic tombs they long to have their names called appreciatively by adults who believe in them and can teach them what they need to make it. These youngsters need to be unwrapped, layer after layer of deep fears, mistrust, basic educational deficiencies, and unawareness of their own resources.

These young men belong to the most feared and despised segment of the American population—poor black males between the ages of 14 and 30. Many of them have turned to drugs, and, when under the influence of drugs, are uncontrollable except by force. Others are so frustrated by their terribly limited prospects that they sit like powder kegs waiting to be ignited. They desperately need help. Phil Davis and his staff try to offer it.

Phil makes two assumptions: we are all about winning, and we the staff are in charge. Does this sound undemocratic, authoritarian? Perhaps, but these boys have had little experience of family life where adults were in charge. Take a simple thing like meals. Most of us take for granted that parents will prepare food for children and that at least once a day a family will sit down and eat it together. These boys are used to getting and eating food whenever they are hungry. Generally they have been accustomed to eat standing up in the kitchen, then leave the dishes where they've used them. They rinse them out when they want to use them again. Although parents from all economic strata report similar behavior by their children, in functioning families there is a certain amount of order to balance the chaos. Some of our youths have been virtually on their own since age four or five. Sociologists call this "family disorganization." It is symptomatic of households where parents are overwhelmed by external problems and interior confusion to the point of dysfunction, even immobility.

To say to adolescent boys "We the staff are in charge" means first of all that "we care enough and we are strong enough to take care of you." "Taking care" does not mean being a hired baby sitter. Rather it means "hanging in" with each boy in daily give and take, sometimes to the point of exhaustion. Taking care means not relinquishing the role of the adult, however provoked.

This is relationship building and parenting at the most fundamental level. When FLOC first opened that group home we made the mistake of expecting the boys to function according to their chronological age rather than their emotional age. We assumed that the boys were ready for a level of teamwork between staff and residents that would take care of food preparation as well as physical and emotional safety. What happened instead was a perpetuation of irregular catch-as-catch-can eating habits, an alarming amount of physical and psychological intimidation of weaker residents by the stronger, and destruction of property. Within a span of weeks a newly remodeled, freshly painted house looked like a slum dwelling.

We realized our mistake and started rebuilding with the same group of adolescents. This time we started at a more elementary level. We hired a cook instead of relying on teams of staff and residents for cooking and meal planning. We insisted that everyone eat together at scheduled times. We made some staff changes and tried to create a physically and psychologically safe environment. One boy, a heavy drug user who had been smuggling drugs into the home, was transferred to a drug treatment center. The other nine stayed put and a new resident was added. Within three months the program stabilized and we were able to start addressing issues higher up the maturity scale, such as assumption of responsibility, development of self-esteem, and learning to verbalize frustrations instead of physically acting them out.

Improvement of academic performance followed. One youth who came in reading at a fourth-grade level tested a year later at the twelfth-grade level. Half of the youngsters increased their reading levels by two to four grades.

These are not dumb kids, but the grave wrappings of past failure and deprivation have to be unwrapped from their intelligence. This requires an environment of order, discipline, high expectations, and encouragement so they can concentrate on intellectual tasks.

THE FLOC LEARNING CENTER

The youths in the group home get their schooling at the FLOC Learning Center, an individualized psycho-educational program for 50 adolescents from ages 12 to 20. These youths have been referred by other FLOC programs, the foster care system, and the public school system because traditional schools can't deal with their acting-out behavior and special needs. Most are poor, all have major gaps in their development. Gwen Mason, a former principal of the Learning Center, said, "For many of these kids this is the only safe, inviting place they experience all day. Some will come here even when they are sick." Teaching these disadvantaged youngsters is nonviolent warfare against the demons they bring with them out of the tomb of chaos. These teachers for a time are the champions of the true destiny of these children. They have to be fighters. They have to motivate and lead the children to take over the ongoing, lifelong struggle for mature personhood.

The compliment that pleases me most in all my over 30 years as Executive Director of FLOC is a remark one school official made to another "Yes, I've heard of FLOC. They really fight for their kids."

Fighting for children and their parents as well as struggling with them—this is what it means to unbind people hungry for a decent life. Another piece of the work is to provide incentives. The children and their parents must have access to a diet sufficiently rich in good things to keep them in the struggle.

HIGH-ENERGY CHOICES

Dr. Betty Watson, researcher for the Urban League, believes that the critical issue in the plight of the poor is the difference between low-energy choices and high-energy choices. This is another way of addressing the issue of empowerment. In the FLOC group home, food changed from a low-energy choice to a high-energy choice as we expected more of ourselves and less of the kids. The staff made mealtime a special time. The food looked good. It smelled good and tasted good. The boys got enthusiastic about eating. They gave up some of their independence, their resistance to the risky process of moving toward belonging, because they wanted the good food. Food moved from being a low priority of the group's life to being a high-energy choice.

The boys became accustomed to quality meals and relationships of mutual trust grew between boys and staff. They were ready for new choices. Then food took its place as a low-energy choice, taken for granted, and they were ready for challenges on a higher level.

Most public policy puts before the poor low-energy choices that the comfortable believe will alleviate their problems. Privileged people expect the poor to appreciate dingy, cramped, rat-infested housing because at least it is shelter and better than exposure to the elements. Likewise, privileged people expect the unemployed to value any kind of employment, because some income must be better than no income. However, for street youths there is always another option—dealing drugs. This can look like a high-energy choice to young people because the payoff is immediate and the rewards many times greater than the effort. They soon learn, however, that the casualty rate from dealing in drugs is high and the street is often one way, leading to prison or death. But by the time they see the drug scene for the cruel, manipulative, exploitive master it is, it may be too late.

Only high-energy choices can call these young people to a healthy, sane, productive life outside the tomb of drugs, violence, and poverty. They need mentors who will walk with them, help them sort out their goals, and encourage them on the journey. To help these children, we must believe there is a future for them as well as ourselves. They need skills, discipline, and awareness so they can move confidently in mainstream society. Organized family life provides these things as a matter of course, and is supplemented by school and community guidance. But even disorganized families can be empowered, and beyond them, whole communities, to provide what young people need.

Family organization in which parents are in charge is only the beginning, but it is crucial. Children learn to exercise authority by internalizing caring parental authority. Fortunate children don't have to take on all the complexities of adult responsibility at once; they can move into it gradually. Unless children internalize authority they will never be able to hold positions of authority in the workplace. They will then be stuck at the entry level positions with pay below the poverty line.

JOB READINESS

Recently I visited the headquarters of a large Washington area retail lumber chain to gather information for developing a FLOC job readiness program. I inquired about their need for entry level personnel, the skills that were required, and the potential for advancement. The company officials said their biggest problems in maintaining a strong work force were workers' impatience and resistance to learning. Entry level workers often perceived the jobs they were assigned as simpler than they really were. After a few weeks on the job they were convinced they had learned enough to move up to a better paying, more responsible position. But often they did not understand the multiple aspects of the job and the importance of each piece. For example, a cashier has to do several things at once: record inventory information on a computerized cash register, figure change, relate positively to a stream of impatient customers, and cope with unexpected demands. Inability to cope in any of these areas requires intervention by the supervisor.

Further, an entry level worker, in addition to demonstrating competence at the current job, has also to convince the supervisor of his/her competence to function at a higher rate of pay. This requires effective use of language and the confidence to negotiate in an assertive, but not aggressive manner.

Any person who has been deprived of dependable adult leadership in the early years has to learn very fast to even gain entry to the fast-paced, competitive world of modern commerce and technology. Justice-minded individuals, churches, and communities can help in this learning as we call entombed children, youths, and adults to freedom.

When we teach, expect, and lead children to win and convey to them that the adults are really there for them, we call them by name to come forth into freedom. The boys in the FLOC group home know this. Slowly, painstakingly, some of these boys are being unbound—maybe most, just possibly all. The process takes time. In the meantime, we who are investing in them are growing ourselves. They are our teachers. They push us to be clear about our own values. By standing up to them and loving them we claim our own manhood and womanhood. By sticking with them in order to unbind them, we are being unbound. It is a joint endeavor, and all who are engaged in it profit.

JOINT LIBERATION WORK

During my Outward Bound course I learned something about this kind of mutual liberation.

On our 26-day course, we kept a very demanding pace day after day. Everyone had to take full responsibility for themselves as well as share responsibility for the group's progress. Every morning we got up with the sun, and while some were cooking breakfast, others were taking down the tents and clearing the campsite. Then we each picked up our own packs and trudged along the trail, or bushwhacked, when there was no trail. Each of us was pushed to our limits. If someone didn't do his or her share, the group suffered.

Many times during that month I didn't think I could go on. After hiking for 12 hours, or after 30 miles of paddling a canoe, I kept going by saying to myself, "Everyone has to carry their own pack—and that means me, age 53 or not." And I looked around at my companions who were also straining and kept going.

The women in the group seemed particularly conscious of this rule. They did not look to a man or even another woman to get their 40-pound packs up on their backs, but learned to swing them on by themselves.

"Everyone carry his or her own pack" was a liberating way of doing things, and yet it had its limits. At times it had to be offset by another rule: we are our brother's or sister's keeper.

Celeste, age 35, worked back home as a secretary. She was not athletic, and had no previous outdoor experience. On our first trek, she was as plucky as anyone, but after a couple of miles of hiking over rocky terrain she fell behind. An instructor fell in step just behind her, encouraging her to keep going.

Another one of our rules was to travel as a group and not let a lot of distance open up between us. Celeste's inability to keep up made this difficult. Our stops became longer and longer. The sun was going down and we wondered if we'd reach our destination that day. During one of the rest stops, a group member said, "Celeste, let us relieve you of some of the weight of your pack and put you next to the leader." Pots, canteen, sleeping bag, poncho were distributed, leaving Celeste with just a few pounds.

Walking next to the leader with a lighter pack, Celeste was able to keep up. The group quickened its pace and arrived at its destination near a mountain stream just as the sun was setting.

The next day we rose early and were on the trail by 6 AM. Celeste was next to the leader. She gamely pushed herself up the narrow mountain trail until we had to negotiate 200 feet of boulders on the mountainside. Celeste was hurting. But there was no turning back. Fellow group members again offered help with the contents of her pack. She accepted. With a lighter pack and the encouragement of Gail, the lead instructor, who talked her over those rocks one at a time, Celeste kept going. After six hours of hiking we reached the top of the mountain. After lunch and a rest, Celeste went around to take back items others had agreed to carry for her. The going would be downhill now and she thought she could manage.

Day by day Celeste's stamina increased. She did not turn into superwoman, but she could hold her own. She cast aside her doubts about finishing the program.

Celeste is a kind of metaphor of empowerment. The more powerful and privileged need not carry the others in a dependent way. They need not rescue the powerless. Only, sometimes, they can offer to share the heavy load. Sometimes those locked into self-defeating behavior and oppressive social structures must have a rope thrown down to them.

And they must respond and catch on. The ones up top need not carve steps in the cliff, but they can provide a rope and some encouragement. They can take some of the poundage of the pack for a while, so that the exhausted or frightened ones have a chance to reach the top, to finish the hike with the whole group.

This is how the more powerful and the least powerful can connect. This is how a fragmented society can be one. This is how the healing can happen. Not that we rescue them, but that we see them, we think about what we can do, we engage, encourage, stand with, enter their world, and invite them to respond.

And they will, some of them. They will leap out for the rope when they do not see any other hand- or footholds. And we on the top come to know that it is us down there on the rock face, or immobile in the wheelchair. And we know that the only way the group is going to get there is if we all go together. We can close the gap between the strong ones walking briskly ahead and the ones who lag behind because their packs are too heavy.

Thus our engagement with the powerless can lead us to unexpected destinations, those we otherwise would have missed. We who apparently have it all can come to know how much we need those who seem weakest.

The friends of Lazarus are transformed, as is Lazarus, in their encounter at the tomb. They have seen the impossible happen—the dead man is alive again. They see possibilities they have never seen before, and their lives can never again slip into the shallowness of self-absorbed living.

Part Three

REFLECTION:
RETHINKING OLD ASSUMPTIONS

Chapter Nine

EXPANDING THE POLITICAL DEBATE

S o far in this book we have considered the plight of the persistently poor in this country through the lens of a Biblical story of transformation. We have been holding together two opposites—the tomblike current reality of persistent poverty and the compelling vision of poor children, adults, and families emerging from that tomb into full participation in a land of opportunity.

In this and following chapters, I am asking my readers to join me in a leap of thought and imagination to envision a breakthrough on a very large scale. The issue of scale is critical. While successful demonstrations of quality services and outcomes are highly significant, the sheer numbers of the persistently poor are too large for us to settle for "good works" here and there. The growing millions of children and adults in poverty challenge us to confront their plight and the country's plight on a large scale, city by city, and across the country. This will involve the complex array of dysfunctional public systems that comprise the so-called American "safety net." It is very clear that our various social service, health, education, housing and other systems and the political processes that shape them are in a state of breakdown. This is beyond debate. The issue on the table is how all of us, citizens and politicians, poor and comfortable, are to make a big enough difference to turn the tide toward a society that works for everyone.

LAZARUS IS ALL OF US

As I put down these thoughts I realize that I am now looking at the Lazarus story from a different angle from where I started. Initially, I read this story with the persistently poor as Lazarus and the rest of us as the healthy community. At this point I am wrestling with Lazarus in the tomb as a symbol of American society. In both a spiritual and practical sense, we are all partially dead, that is, shut off from our fullest selves by entrenched spiritual, psychological, and structural barriers. We as a country stand in need of liberation to become the land of opportunity we believe it our call and destiny to be. The call into the tomb to the dead man, "Come forth, Lazarus," is addressed also to this country, to us collectively as well as to each person individually.

I write out of a deep commitment to the American vision of an inclusive society where children born in circumstances of poverty have a fair shot at becoming confident, competent adults who are able to support themselves and contribute to the common good. I write, as well as work day to day in the trenches at For Love of Children, to contribute to this eventual outcome. I also write to gain the upper hand in my struggle with despair. I too am Lazarus.

I have worked at the same job in the same city for over 30 years. Over the last 10 years, I have seen the situation of poor children and families worsen considerably. At times I ask myself, "What's the use?" In those times it seems that the cynics may be right, that this country and especially its cities are in irreversible decline. Then the better side of me rallies and says, "There is another reality here." Even if one-fourth of the city's youth are dropping out of school, having babies while still children, turning to guns and violence, three-fourths of the city's low income youth are doing the right things under very discouraging conditions. They go to school. They treat others with respect. They refrain from stealing. They aspire to personal goals.

I believe there is some kind of divine human struggle going on here. I believe that God is in this struggle, and that God is on the side of life; that God has the last word, and that word is grace and not condemnation. Dag Hammarskjold said, "We are surrounded by grace." I write to uncover the dimension of hope and possibility, the sense of God on our side as well as God standing over and against us calling us to account. I write to pull together a mental frame that enables me to stay on course in the face of my own and my colleagues' propensity to resignation.

CHANGING THE WAY WE THINK

For the rest of this book I intend to challenge the despair and resignation of people like myself, who care, but wonder how it is possible for ordinary folks to make a difference. I do not see a guru out there who knows how to "fix" persistent poverty. I submit that we don't have to be experts to contribute to a groundswell for large scale social change. I believe we need to change our accustomed ways of thinking.

However, to begin this conversation, three things must happen. First, we must suspend disbelief. A conversation that awakens awareness of possibility does not happen when people are stuck in resignation and disbelief. Possibility cannot show up; it does not emerge into consciousness, in a climate of disbelief, resignation, and cynicism. Secondly, we must learn the art of envisioning—that is, inventing mental pictures of a desired future. A vision is a picture someone invents in her or his head and then gives it the possibility of life by speaking the vision to others.

Thirdly, we must uncover language that communicates the vision in ways that enable people with diverse interests to really hear one another, find common ground, and have powerful conversations that lead to breakthrough ideas and action.

BREAKTHROUGH THINKING

A breakthrough in thinking involves substituting a positive mental/emotional outlook for the all-too-familiar negative mindset of despair. This creates a clearing for possibility. It creates space for freshness, for getting out of the box shaped by the past. It starts with what Paul Tillich called "the courage to be." A useful description of faith is *standing in the future in the face of no agreement.*[1] This kind of stance opens the door to possibility, while resignation shuts that door.

The level of agreement around changing the tomblike structures and psychology of persistent poverty is low at the present time. Most people, like the media, are so fixated on the problems and finding someone to blame for the problems that there is little space for conversation toward invention. The pain-driven mentality of reaction and complaint crowds out creative thinking.

We need to make distinctions between faith and resignation and being and nonbeing. These distinctions enable us to think about possibility that goes beyond the recognizable.

Webster's Dictionary defines miracle as "an extraordinary event in the physical world which surpasses all *known* [italics mine] human or natural powers and is ascribed to a supernatural cause." This definition is sufficiently broad to arguably include such historic events as the fall of the Berlin Wall, the collapse of the communist empire in eastern Europe, and the dismantling of the apartheid system in South Africa. No one was publicly predicting these huge transitional events to occur when they did. Nonetheless they happened, because many individuals had been standing, speaking, acting with that future in mind *in the face of no agreement*. Because of their contribution, the ground was fertile for transformation that went beyond expectation. Moreover, even though each of these revolutions has had complicated aftermaths, possibility for the future has been created that was not there before.

I invite you to consider the possibility that persistent poverty in both the United States and the world is no more and no less given by the past than east European communism and South African apartheid and no more and no less subject to change, given even a relatively few standing, speaking, and acting an alternative vision. Make no mistake, it will take a social, economic, and political shift as huge as the shift from communism and apartheid to democracy to break through the now well established trend in the U.S. toward deepening poverty for the children, women, and men in the poorest 20% of the population. That is reality. Persistent poverty is both economic and psychological, both structural and the product of bad collective and individual choices. Economic poverty is also the product of the spiritual poverty of individuals and a society with unused ability to distinguish between faith and resignation, between being and nonbeing, and to see the connection between the common good and long term economic prosperity.

THE ENCOUNTER BETWEEN
VISION AND REALITY

We have been holding together two opposites—the vision of an inclusive society and the reality of increasing, persistent poverty. Between vision and reality there is an inherent structural tension. We deal with this tension in one of two ways. One choice is to reduce it by either denying the reality or surrendering the vision. The other choice is to stand in the structural tension between vision and reality and allow the tension to spur us toward a better outcome. If and when we reach a new outcome we are confronted by a new structural tension, and face the same set of choices again. So life goes, and this challenge makes it interesting.

The following diagram illustrates this human situation.[2]

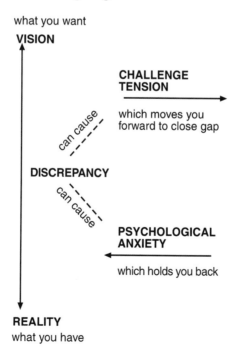

One of the purposes of this book is to explore language and perspective that open the possibility of a generative conversation between people of diverse political, social, and religious orientations. By *generative,* I mean a conversation that moves beyond debate aimed at proving one side right and the other wrong to a dialogue that unconceals possibilities. This only occurs when participants are listening and speaking to each other out of their listening. The word *generative* suggests a capacity of producing offspring, of productivity that leads to further productivity.

The choice to stand in the tension between vision and reality applies to every individual, group, organization, institution, and society. It goes with the territory of being alive, of being human. This is the playing field of possibility. The other choice is resignation and cynicism. On that field the only game is a holding action, to resist change in order to hold on to what one has or to keep things from getting worse.

EXAMINING THE EXISTING
POLITICAL DEBATE

The 1980s and 1990s have meant deepening poverty for the women, children, and minority men in the bottom 20% of the U.S. population, escalating wealth for the predominantly white top 20%, and a standstill for the middle 60%. Traditional liberals say that the solution to this problem is to redistribute income through tax policy and expand government programs for the benefit of those left behind. Traditional conservatives say the solution is to stimulate the economy through lower taxes, reduce the size of government and the scope of government intervention, and return to a true free enterprise system.

Since World War II, we have successively attempted each of these alternatives, tilting toward the liberal alternative in the 1960s and 70s, and shifting strongly toward conservatism in the 1980s. The 1990s find us in the kind of paralysis described by Lisbeth Schorr:

"Many Americans have soured on 'throwing money' at human problems that seem only to get worse. They are not hard-hearted, but don't want to be soft-headed either. Even when their compassion is aroused by moving stories of desperate families or neglected children, they feel helpless and are convinced that nothing can be done. Fear of actually doing harm while trying to do good, together with the threat of unmanageable costs, have paralyzed national policies."[3]

THE LIMITS OF THE
CURRENT POLITICAL DEBATE

The current political debate in the U.S. takes place within the narrow space between two familiar poles, traditional liberalism and traditional conservatism. It is interesting that despite their considerable differences, both liberals and conservatives take a common approach to persistent poverty—i.e., they both acknowledge it as a problem, and then blame it on different causes. Conservatives generally assume that the individual, the parents, or the grandparents were irresponsible, or that they failed to socialize their children properly. While conservatives focus on the individual and the loss of traditional values, liberals generally blame an unjust or dysfunctional system, and assume that greedy, entrenched political and economic interests are depriving the poor of social justice.

Because they see the individual at the root of the problem of poverty, conservatives are skeptical of government intervention. They typically argue that the side effects of government programs more often than not cancel out their good intentions. For example, they claim that the welfare system shifts responsibility from the individual to society, creating an incentive to laziness.

Liberals are generally optimistic about the potential good of government intervention. They typically argue that government programs more often than not prevent social disaster. They say a "laissez faire" economy is not sufficiently self-corrective to deal with disruptions like plant closings, or the country's shift from a farm/heavy industry economy to an information driven economy, much less the myriad personal misfortunes that can occur.

Each side sees only a part of the picture. Conservatives typically ignore the human consequences of a single-minded reliance on free enterprise, and liberals typically fail to acknowledge market cycles and the crucial role of economic innovation. The newspaper and television media reinforce this narrow debate by making it appear that there are really only two basic choices for political direction—conservative or liberal, as defined by the recent past. What goes unsaid is how alike are these political poles.

Both are problem-driven and therefore blame-oriented. Both, like the media, focus on what is wrong and who is to blame, and propose short term solutions.

EXAMINING UNDERLYING ASSUMPTIONS IN THE EXISTING DEBATE

The term *paradigm* suggests a pattern of thinking that people who think that way assume to be a given. It is thus generally the case that when people who stand in different paradigms have a conversation, they speak past each other. They only hear in terms of what fits within or outside their particular paradigm. Their listening is contaminated by the already active conversation in their brains, to the point that they engage more in debate than in conversation. The outcome is reinforcement of past ways of thinking rather than discovery of new possibility.

TRADITIONAL LIBERAL ASSUMPTIONS

Drexel Sprecher, leadership educator and political philosopher, has some helpful things to say about the underlying assumptions that shape the existing political debate.[4]

Sprecher perceives in the traditional liberal arguments an underlying paradigm that he calls an *unconstrained rational paradigm.* This paradigm derives from the basic assumption that the world is rationally ordered, or at least orderable. Organized society is like a machine, in which social problems like poverty result from malfunctions. If we understand how society is malfunctioning and fix it, then it will run like it is supposed to—that is, for the benefit of the common good.

Liberalism thus assumes that reality is inherently rational, and that the economic, social, political, and personal forces that drive the evolution of society can be changed and controlled through scientific intervention. We may have to wait for a solution, but eventually we will figure it out and fix our problems, provided we have enough political will to stay the course. Given this *unconstrained* assessment of reality, liberalism is inherently optimistic about the human ability to solve social problems—whether they be unemployment, poverty, housing, cancer, AIDS, or war. Poverty exists because of irrational conditions that have developed over time, such as the unfair advantage that time-honored institutions like the free market have given to powerful interests. Wrest control from oppressive vested interests, redistribute political power, and social problems like poverty will be solved.

Liberals believe that human nature is good, or at least neutral. Human institutions can therefore be designed rationally, according to a scientific model. Liberal thinkers see the cause of evil as institutions dominated by power elites—the free market, the military-industrial complex, and even organized religion.

TRADITIONAL CONSERVATIVE ASSUMPTIONS

Conservatives start from the opposite assumption: the world is inherently chaotic, and the underlying economic, social, and personal forces at play in human affairs are therefore fundamentally uncontrollable. Conservatives perceive human nature to be inherently self-centered and competitive. Because human nature is the way it is, the benefits of collective action are mixed at best. As conservatives see poverty, for example, the forces that feed it cannot be controlled by political action, and therefore, poverty for some is unavoidable. The best we can do is to minimize disincentives to hard work, provide deterrents to laziness and disorderly behavior, and concentrate upon helping those who are willing to help themselves.

Conservatives assume limited possibilities, and liberals assume unlimited possibilities. Hence Sprecher describes the underlying conservative pattern of thinking as a *constrained rational paradigm* in contrast to the unconstrained rational paradigm assumed by liberals. Conservatives say that you cannot gather enough information about a situation as complex as the economy, or exercise enough control at a distance to rationally order society better than the market can. Thus they limit the use of reason to individual choices about particular situations, and oppose centralized or governmental efforts to tamper with the market. The market should be left alone so the "invisible hand" of free enterprise can work.

Conservatives readily agree that the free market system isn't perfect, but claim it doesn't have to work perfectly to work better than government intervention. The free enterprise system has produced a higher standard of living for more people than any other economic system. And conservatives believe that, in the long run, uninhibited free enterprise will benefit the poor more than expensive government programs. As they see it, government interventions create new problems for each one they partially ameliorate. Thus, while liberals attempt to rationally solve, conservatives attempt to rationally contain or mitigate the irrational.

CREDITS AND LIABILITIES OF
THE EXISTING DEBATE

Both liberalism and conservatism have something to offer. Each has a limited range of useful application. Liberals tell us that we do not have to settle for society in its current condition. They can point to real advances through government initiative—the dismantling of legalized racial segregation through court decisions and civil rights legislation, a dramatic reduction in the numbers of elderly poor through the social security system, and the rapid expansion of the middle class through the educational opportunities created by the GI Bill at the close of World War II and student loan funds in recent years.

Liberals recall with pride the activist administration of Franklin D. Roosevelt. When Roosevelt came into office in 1933, U.S. unemployment was 25 percent. He put Harry Hopkins in charge of putting people back to work immediately through public jobs. Roosevelt despised welfare. Working in an unheated office, Hopkins started on November 2, 1933. By November 23, he had 800,000 people working. Two weeks later, that total had grown to two million. During the seven years the Works Progress Administration (WPA) was in existence, 1935 to 1941, WPA workers built more than 650,000 miles of highways, roads and sidewalks, 124,000 bridges, 39,000 schools, and 125,000 other public buildings. The total seven year cost of the WPA for these benefits to the country in 1991 dollars was $90 billion. This country, which was relatively undeveloped at the time, made the investment in money and political and administrative energy. Millions of families were preserved and the country held together when many were losing faith in our democratic system.[5]

Many conservatives do not oppose government initiative per se. What they fear is the way government attempts to solve one problem disrupt social processes and create other problems. For example, the welfare system has prevented millions of destitute mothers from losing their children, but it has become a dehumanizing trap for the women and children it was created to assist. Conservatives typically see bringing down the inflation rate as contributing more to the diminishment of poverty than government-initiated direct service programs. If government will get out of the way, they believe, the American economic system is sufficiently dynamic to provide jobs for all who want to work. It is then the job of the schools, churches, and private institutions to foster the traditional values of self-discipline, high goals, and hard work that will bring the people left behind into the mainstream.

While each side of the existing political debate has something to offer, the success and applicability of each of these respective ways of thinking has been partial. For example, liberal civil rights legislation did not achieve racial inclusion because it did not deal with racism, or to be more precise, the ideology of white supremacy. The underlying assumption was that if you change the structures, attitudinal changes will follow. But the ideology of white supremacy is not rational.

Moreover, the social security system, perhaps the most widely supported of all liberal initiatives, remains a limited solution as long as a diminishing percentage of current workers pay to cover expanding benefits for more and more retirees. The social security system has evolved from a liberal intervention into an institution that resists change as much as any conservative institution. By opposing this system's further evolution, liberals and conservatives alike limit the realization of new possibilities.

In sum, neither the liberal nor the conservative paradigm is complete enough to see emerging possibilities and convert those possibilities into successful action that moves society forward. We need new, more open-ended ways of thinking; hence the need for new paradigms.

NEW PARADIGMS

Sprecher maintains that at least two alternative paradigms are now emerging to compete with the unconstrained rational and constrained rational paradigms that underlie the existing political debate. He calls these *the living systems paradigm* and the *generative paradigm.*

The basic assumption of the living systems paradigm is that the world is an evolving organism with an inner momentum toward betterment. This contrasts with the mechanical view of reality in the liberal paradigm and the chaotic view of reality in the conservative paradigm. Whereas traditional liberals assume that we can change the forces that drive evolution and traditional conservatives assume that we cannot change those forces but only contain them, the living systems paradigm assumes that we can *work with* these forces. Consequently, what liberals and conservatives perceive as social problems that need fixing or containment, the living systems paradigm perceives as evidence of breakdown and a push towards further evolution. Noxious conditions such as high unemployment, persistent poverty, and the drug epidemic pile up because individuals, institutions, and society *are resisting change and evolution.*

The generative paradigm goes a step further, positing that the forces that play out in human affairs are rooted in *consciousness.* This means that aspirations and ideals, what goes on inside the heart and spirit of a people, inevitably generates actions and social structures. From a generative paradigm perspective, history is a series of experiments directed toward realizing these aspirations and ideals in civilization.

Consider how the aspirations and ideals incorporated in the Declaration of Independence have played out in the evolution of this country. "We hold these truths to be self-evident, that all men are endowed by their creator with certain inalienable rights. Among these are life, liberty, and the pursuit of happiness." These ideals, which at first applied only to property-holding white males, fueled a political revolt toward nationhood and away from colonial status. Decades later these ideals gave rise to universal suffrage. They continue to work in the evolution of national consciousness with regard to women and minorities. Perhaps next we will see that they also apply to children.

With apologies to Sprecher, I am merging the living systems paradigm with the generative paradigm and calling the combination a *generative orientation*. I do so because the fundamental distinction I want to make is between the similarity of the traditional liberal and conservative unconstrained and constrained rational paradigms and the very different option of a generative orientation.

On the surface, liberal and conservative thinking appear to be opposites. Conservatism is driven by a kind of social Darwinism that sees life as a competitive struggle for survival. Competition is necessary because of scarcity. Moreover, competition develops the discipline to make maximum use of resources and thereby gives the best overall outcome. Liberalism stresses the value of cooperation over competition. It emphasizes equality and collective responsibility, in contrast to the conservative emphasis on the individual and the family. For the liberal, the prime social goal is justice, understood as the equal distribution of opportunity, which is connected to the equal distribution of power. For the conservative, the prime goal is individual freedom, understood as the least possible interference by government consistent with public safety.

While approaching issues quite differently, traditional liberals and conservatives actually share a common remedial orientation. They basically react to the pain in society and define it as a problem which they seek to change (liberal) or contain (conservative). They both operate through competition and coercion. They are opposite sides of the same coin, and in the existing narrow political debate each functions to limit the other.

The generative orientation is very different. According to the generative orientation, every noxious condition in society carries within it an *evolutionary intent*. That is to say, behind and within the noxious condition is an evolutionary thrust toward betterment. An example is teen pregnancy. A generative orientation challenges us to recognize the natural craving of adolescent girls to be acknowledged and valued participants in the world. This is the *evolutionary intent*. Therefore, to assist adolescent girls, we have to look behind their sexual activity to their aspirations. Producing a baby is in these instances a counterproductive way of fulfilling evolutionary intent. But if we can address the evolutionary intent, then teenage decision-making, which now leads to early pregnancy and often to social dependency, will evolve toward betterment.

The generative orientation challenges us to recognize and work with the underlying forces of evolution in society. It assumes, in contrast to liberals, that we cannot change these forces; and, in contrast to conservatives, that we do not have to settle for containing these forces. Instead of either assumption, generative thinking assumes that *we can work with these forces*. It assumes that the economic, social, political, and personal forces are too strong and independent to be changed and too resilient and reactive to be contained. Our goal must be to recognize, respect, understand, and utilize the energy of these forces to assist society's and the individual's evolution. Joanna Macy says, "You cannot fix the world, but you can take part in its self-healing."[6]

In an important way, the generative orientation represents a view of evolution that is more complex than the unconstrained and constrained rational paradigms. In this orientation, reality is multi-dimensional. It includes spirit as well as mind, and it is much more dynamic than logic itself can account for. It accounts for culture as well as politics and expands the narrow focus of the liberal/conservative remedial orientation.

The liberal era, which began two centuries ago with the development of the scientific method, moved humankind beyond the middle ages and their rigid hierarchical structures, dominated by the alliance between Church and landholding class. The elevation of rationalism, the hallmark of liberalism, permitted a rapid social and economic diversification of society and the emergence of the individual.

At this moment in human history, liberal and conservative institutions and processes, which were creative in an earlier time, are breaking down. And often the cost of maintaining liberal and conservative institutions exceeds their benefit. Liberal-initiated government institutions, such as public welfare, child welfare, public education, and public housing systems have become seriously dysfunctional. Costs are high, outcomes are unsatisfactory, and discontent is widespread. The conservative alternative of turning social responsibility over to the private sector and expecting an unleashed free market and volunteerism to create all the jobs, housing, medical care, and children's services that are needed has not worked either.

Generative thinking starts with the question— What do we want? This is a very different starting place than "What is wrong?" or "What must we protect?" The key question in generative thinking is: What is intrinsically significant? The answer is the clue to the direction of evolution toward betterment. For example, with regard to health care, the fundamental questions are "What is wellness?" and "How do we evolve toward it?" That is a very different approach than asking "What is the disease?" "What is causing it?" or "How do we cure it?" According to generative thinking, fresh energy emerges when we move toward a goal of intrinsic worth, such as wellness. Singlemindedly fighting the disease leads to burnout, but a generative approach releases energy that keeps growing, making way for the Biblical promise of "running and not getting weary, of walking and not fainting" within the context of striving for whole new systems.

A generative process transforms inputs of time, material, intellect, spirit, love, work, and vision into a whole that is greater than the sum of its parts. Generative thinking assumes that change is a constant (and presupposes continuing adaptation by individual and society). In short, evolution is ongoing. Even good institutions must evolve or else become impediments to the creative flow of evolution.

In the generative view, it is possible not only to work with the dynamic forces that operate in human affairs, but to engage with those forces from within, at the level of consciousness. Ideals, purposes, and goals which are of intrinsic value can become powerful instruments of change by being articulated in the form of vision. Vision, by definition, is always beyond our current reach. Nonetheless, a compelling vision sets a direction, and it can engage the consciousness of other individuals, institutions, and the whole society. By penetrating individual and collective consciousness, the vision works from within to transform consciousness, which then can drive social change.

In the generative orientation, the primary mode of knowing is intuition. This contrasts with the rational mode of the liberal and conservative paradigms. But vision and rational planning are not opposed to each other. Both are essential, but we must start from vision—i.e., a clear mental picture of the desired outcome.

In the generative orientation, a compelling vision engages the economic, social, political, and personal forces at work in human affairs from within. This vision taps into deep wells of consciousness because it pictures what is intrinsically worthwhile, our deepest human longings. Both liberal and conservative goal-setting tend to miss these longings because goals are stated in terms of solving or mitigating a problem. But vision cannot be expressed in terms of the problem. The goal of reducing poverty by 50% is based on viewing poverty as a problem, but the goal of creating a trained workforce—able to compete with other developed nations, evolving intensive worldwide trade, and showing a high ratio of output to cost—is based on a vision of what is intrinsically worthwhile.

So vision sets a direction for action. The next step is to scale down or "miniaturize" the vision into a form that is doable within a limited time frame. Scaling down the vision lets us experiment toward the vision. This requires rational planning, but the planning is shaped by the vision rather than by the problem. Momentum and energy develop with the successful completion of action.

In the generative orientation, many pieces of action fit together by their *alignment with a common vision*. It is the alignment of immediate actions with vision that catalyzes progress toward betterment. In the generative orientation, the world is a hologram with multiple, simultaneous processes, all projecting consciousness and driving or restricting evolution.

FROM A LIBERAL-CONSERVATIVE TO A GENERATIVE-REMEDIAL DEBATE

Because liberalism and conservatism share a common remedial orientation, in the existing narrow political debate each functions to limit the other. In three consecutive Presidential elections (1980, 84, 88) this country elected a conservative President (Ronald Reagan and George Bush) and a liberal Congress. In the mid-term election of 1994 and presidential election of 1996, the election shifted the other way. One might say that, for lack of a larger vision, the voting public inadvertently pits two coercive paradigms against each other and thereby keeps things from moving very far in either direction. The operation of government is balanced around the status quo. As generative thinking interprets reality, a government balanced around the status quo is not an agent for substantial evolution. Tradeoffs, rather than evolution or transformation, define what will happen, and individual responsibility is eroded as people look to government for solutions that are too complex for government alone to accomplish.

The generative orientation assumes that energy develops as an individual or organization pursues the path of a compelling vision. By focusing on possibilities, the generative orientation sees experimentation and learning by trial and error as critical to progress. The generative orientation looks at dysfunction as a sign of unavoidable breakdown and decay; a major task then is to discern the generative dimension of that which is ineffective or harmful. In the generative orientation, progressing institutions and persons are always moving between realizing their ideals and confronting both what is missing and what gets in the way. The necessity of change is a constant. We have to be ready to relinquish processes that worked in an earlier situation but not in the new. This means that significant energy and resources of a generative institution, social system, or individual will be committed to thinking from the future rather than the past and to experimentation.

Whereas the driving force of the remedial orientation is either the competitive individual or the collective force of a government or institution, the driving force of the generative orientation is an individual or group committed to bringing something to realization, and being accountable for engaging the world in the process. The individual is not in a win/lose competition with others, as in the Darwinian conservative paradigm, but seeks to draw in others to realize a broad goal. The generative orientation shares with the liberal paradigm a commitment to the common good, but it does not rely on a consensus with others in order to act. The generative individual commits to bring something to realization because of its intrinsic worth. Other stakeholders are engaged by a compelling case strong and clear enough to attract their support. Forward energy does not wait upon consensus.

The individual assuming responsibility out of a generative orientation is not obsessed with solutions. Instead, such a leader would look at the forces operating in a situation (rather than the ineffective situation itself) and then try to work with these forces to release more effective behavior. Because social processes are generally too complex to be rationally planned from start to finish, it is most effective to set a clear direction and then to experiment toward it, incorporating feedback from the experience into an evolving process of action and reflection. A narrow and rigid adherence to a pre-set plan rules out new possibilities that occur on the way.

Just as remedial thinking is obsessed with solutions, it also places great weight on hope. Generative thinking is tolerant of the dynamics of hopelessness. There are often times when individuals and groups are confronted with the death or irreversible lifelessness of old structures, ideas, processes, and relationships. New life, new energy can only come by letting go of the familiar, and bravely looking to the empty, unformed future as the place of possibility. In this way the giving up of hope as a longing for restoration of the past becomes a powerful step toward empowerment. Holding on to ineffective processes protects individuals and the society from the disequilibrium necessary to entertain new possibilities. Generative thinking withdraws energy from that which is manifestly not working, to sit in the hopelessness long enough to discern the aspiration at work beneath the breakdown, and to discover how to work with those dynamic energies. It may be that we are currently going through this process as a country.

Chapter Ten

APPLYING NEW PARADIGMS TO GRASSROOTS ACTION

Eliminating persistent poverty is an exceedingly complex challenge. The multidimensional Lazarus story points to the complexity—rolling away the structural barriers, calling the isolated into community, waiting for the dead to hear their names and answer the call to life, and unbinding the shackles of the past. Each piece is critical to the whole. Leave out any one and the process stalls.

We are using the Lazarus story as metaphor for the transformation of persons and systems, which is tied into the transformation of cities, the country, and indeed the whole interconnected world. Poverty represents a breakdown, a disconnect. Concentrations of poverty represent a big breakdown, huge disconnects.

How can we conceive resolving the breakdown and mending the disconnect? How can finite people and organizations, public and private, hope to contribute to change that is so complex and far reaching? Do we have to conceive the How to contribute to betterment, to make a difference? No.

Small scale actions do make a difference, provided they support the ultimate goal. In fact, small scale actions prepare the way for large scale change, which cannot occur until enough knowledge and experience have accumulated.

INSIGHTS FROM THE NEW SCIENCE

It is refreshing to read Margaret J. Wheatley's description in *Leadership and the New Science* of how our understanding of the universe is being radically altered by the "new science"—the revolutionary discoveries in quantum physics, chaos theory, and biology that are overturning the models that dominated science for centuries. Newtonian physics separated things into parts and posited that action is a direct result of force exerted from one particle to another. Quantum physics perceives a world where relationship is the key determiner of how particles manifest themselves. It sees unseen connections between what were previously thought to be separate entities. Whole populations of a species can shift their behavior because of collective accumulations of knowledge, not because they individually have taken the time to learn new behavior.

Wheatley says, "I believe the evolving emphasis in our society to 'think globally, act locally' expresses a quantum perception of reality. Acting locally is a sound strategy for changing large systems. Instead of trying to map an elaborate system, the advice is to work with the system that you know, one you can get your arms around. Acting locally allows us to work with the movement and flow of simultaneous events within that small system. We are more likely to become synchronized with that system, and thus to have an impact. Those changes in small places, however, create large-system changes, not because they build upon one another, but because they share in the unbroken wholeness that has united them all along. Our activities in one part of the whole create non-local causes that emerge far from us. There is value in working with the system any place it manifests because unseen connections will create effects at a distance, in places we never thought."[1]

In Chapter Nine, we distinguished the remedial orientation that underlies the traditional liberal-conservative political debate and the generative alternative. How might these two orientations manifest in the real operations of actual programs and in advocacy for social change? How do they speak to the issues of scale and complexity?

LESSONS LEARNED IN THE
CLOSING OF JUNIOR VILLAGE

When I heard on a bright summer afternoon in 1973 that the last group of children had left Junior Village and the institution had closed, I took the day off. We had worked for eight years for this outcome. I wanted some time to myself to savor it, and to think about the process.

There was much to celebrate. A group of citizens had taken on a complex social problem in our community and made a difference. We had taken away an option that allowed the child welfare system to procrastinate and drift in its responsibility to the city's most needy children and families. The chief selling points for Junior Village had been its convenience and its presumed ability to ensure children's safety. Martin Fields, a courageous Junior Village staff member, blew the whistle on institutional abuse, carefully documenting persistent patterns of sexual and physical abuse of weaker children by stronger children with the knowledge of staff and without their intervention. Junior Village was not a safe place for children. Moreover, its convenience for child placement contributed to a pattern of delay in resolving the complex issues of family reunification or placement for adoption. Many children lost contact with their parents and siblings, and drifted in the system until permanent foster care became the only option. The average length of stay in the system grew steadily until it reached an average of seven years, close to the highest in the nation.

The decision to close the institution, however, left much to be desired. Mayor Walter Washington had been backed into a corner by aggressive community advocacy and the relentless spotlight of *The Washington Post,* which kept the story before the public for over six months. City Council member Stanley Anderson introduced legislation mandating the closing of Junior Village over a two-year period, forbidding the placement of any child under six in any future public institution, and requiring the Department of Public Welfare to develop a comprehensive plan for alternative child and family services. The legislation passed with only one dissenting vote. Junior Village had become a political liability.

Within a year of its closing, however, the Department of Public Welfare assigned staff to locate space for a successor institution to Junior Village that could handle 100 children on an emergency basis. No action was forthcoming on the development of a comprehensive plan of alternative services.

When news of the initiative to open a successor institution surfaced, FLOC filed a lawsuit to require the Department to fulfill the City Council legislation. Rather than fight the case in court, the Department discontinued its effort to establish a second Junior Village and set up a task force to develop a comprehensive service plan. A year later the Department presented a 300-page wish list of programs with no order of priority or timetable and a budget so high that it was immediately clear they were not serious about implementation. There was no vision for a new system. There was only the expansion and some rearrangement of the old system. I wondered if after winning a battle, we were losing the war.

The goal of those of us working from the outside was the transformation of the District of Columbia child welfare system from a last ditch, child rescue operation to a prevention-oriented system that develops family and community capacity to prevent abuse and neglect and to intervene quickly and skillfully when it occurs. Many in the bureaucracy were committed to the same vision. Unfortunately, policy and direction were dictated by immediate problems, perceived to be crises, with scarce energy or resources for innovation and long term solutions. The system was essentially pain-driven rather than vision-driven, and there is no way to get ahead of the curve from a predominantly reactive stance.

FLOC OPENS A CHILD ADVOCACY CENTER

By this time it was clear that the work of system change, whether initiated from the inside or outside, requires enormous persistence, in-depth knowledge of the complex structures and processes of the child welfare system, and exceptional skills of communication. To sustain the effort, FLOC set up a Child Advocacy Center with a two-person staff and a cadre of 25 volunteers. The Center was funded by grants from the Eugene and Agnes Meyer and Edna McConnell Clark Foundations and many small contributors. Dr. Ann Maney involved the National Institute of Mental Health in directing some of their research capacity to analyze the District of Columbia child welfare system and its implications for mental health. The input of Dr. Maney's office plus the legal and budget analysis and community organizing skills of Elizabeth Dyson, Mary Ann Stein, Nancy Smith, and Ellen Griffith made the Center a very sophisticated operation. It was one of the first child advocacy centers in the country. It took on issues that are now coming prominently into public view—balancing parents' rights and children's rights, how to conceptualize a system of many parts working in alignment, tradeoffs between intensive in-home services and out-of-home placements of children, and updating legal codes and public policy to conform to a family-focused philosophy and commitment.

During its 10 year existence from 1973 to 1983, when it closed for lack of funding, the FLOC Child Advocacy Center generated two important pieces of legislation for the District of Columbia, a bill authorizing subsidies for people who adopt physically and mentally handicapped children, and the DC Prevention of Child Abuse and Neglect Act, which overhauled the outdated codes governing the DC child welfare system. Each year the Center provided a careful analysis of the DC budget and its implications for children and families to the Mayor, City Council, and citizens during the annual city budget setting process. It generated and sustained a lively child advocacy coalition of over 50 organizations, which made its presence felt on children's issues.

The closing of Junior Village was a forward step, but it soon became clear that unless that step was part of a holistic process of change, the process would turn back on itself. Improved possibilities for children in foster homes are quickly undermined without standards, training, and monitoring that move the system toward quality care. If effective work is not done to strengthen families and keep out-of-home placement of children to cases where it is truly necessary, the system will continue to overload, creating a rising demand for foster homes that becomes impossible to fulfill. Moreover, without a shared vision, the cost savings created by the closing of expensive institutional care will be siphoned off to resolve other city crises. All of the above happened, and the system continued in its traditional reactive course for 20 more years, until a class action lawsuit launched another attempt at reform which is now underway.

HARD QUESTIONS

From time to time over the last three decades I have asked myself, "Are we accomplishing any more than holding a finger in the dike? Is system change really possible? How does a community get out of the downward spiral of problems breeding problems? How do we get ahead of the curve? How does a community achieve a public-private partnership with a shared vision and enough clout to make a difference?" It was years later that I realized I was beginning to distinguish the remedial and generative orientations.

Abused and neglected children and their families are as much at risk of being damaged by the system set up to protect and heal them as by the circumstances of their lives. The state is ill equipped to be a parent. State systems are so complex that children removed from their birth families often lose contact with parents, brothers, sisters, and relatives. As adults they have to piece together who they are and where they have come from on their own.

A CLOSED SYSTEM

Through this process I became keenly aware of what sociologists call "closed systems," a category that includes bureaucracies operating out of a pain-driven, remedial orientation. Because its highest value was maintaining equilibrium and avoiding blame, the DC child welfare system carefully controlled input into its decision-making. It invited the community's assistance in meeting specific needs, such as foster parent recruitment, but not in developing a shared vision for the system.

The American Heritage Dictionary defines equilibrium: "1. A condition in which the results of all acting influences are canceled by others, resulting in a stable, balanced, or unchanging system. 2. Physics. The condition of a system in which the resultant of all acting forces is zero ...".

Wheatley says that equilibrium is the tendency of closed systems to wear down, to give off energy that can never be retrieved. "In classical thermodynamics, equilibrium is the end state in the evolution of isolated systems, the point at which the system has exhausted all of its capacity for change, done its work, and dissipated its productive capacity into useless entropy. (Entropy is an inverse measure of a system's capacity for change. The more entropy there is, the less the system is capable of changing.) At equilibrium, there is nothing left for the system to do; it can produce nothing more."[2]

Generative thinking offers an alternative. Open systems have the possibility of continuously importing energy from the environment and of exporting entropy. Open systems don't sit quietly by as their energy dissipates. Instead they maintain a state of non-equilibrium, "keeping the system off balance so that it can change and grow. They participate in an active exchange with their world, using what is there for their own renewal. Every organism in nature, including us, behaves in this way."[3]

THE FLOC LEARNING CENTER

One of the most difficult populations to serve in our city is hostile, alienated adolescents. In the Learning Center, a therapeutic day school, FLOC reaches out to 50 youths identified by the public school and foster care systems as "emotionally disturbed" or "learning disabled" (ED, LD). These youths bring enormous unfocused anger about negative conditions in their lives and environments outside the school. Because they have not learned to recognize and deal with their anger, they unleash it at their peers and their teachers at the slightest provocation. This persistent "in your face" behaviour confronts staff constantly with the distinctions between the remedial and generative orientations. To be effective with children in this state of development, staff must learn how to deal with them out of a generative orientation—keeping in mind that somewhere aspirations for growth and relationship are alive in the youth—even when his or her behavior has to be contained by physical restraint. Bottled-up rage must be vented sufficiently to enable the student to concentrate on the task at hand, but not allowed to trigger a chain reaction in the other students. And the staff must stay directed toward the vision of coaching students who have the self-control of three-year-olds to give up old patterns and learn better ones.

On one particularly stressful day, the Learning Center's Director, Gail Hilliard-Nelson, called a meeting for staff to deal with their mounting outrage at verbal abuse from students. One teacher spoke for the others, "This behavior has got to stop! These kids cannot be allowed to abuse us. Give them a choice: 'Shape up or ship out.'"

In an instant, they were involved in dialogue between the remedial and generative orientations discussed in the previous chapter. The conservative "law and order" approach was surely appealing. It is impossible for education to take place in chaos. The chaos the students bring in from their confused lives has to be contained. The unconstrained rational view that their behaviour is symptomatic of oppressive societal structures, while less appealing in the midst of conflict, is also relevant. The bottom line issue is: How do we use this particular day to make a difference to these deeply hurting and hurtful children?

Staff members all knew that these children are much more familiar with being abused and abusing others than with being treated and treating with respect. That is why they are in the Learning Center. They also knew that self-control and mutual respect cannot be forced, only taught and modeled. How could this staff connect with hidden positive forces in the youths?

After a half hour of ventilation, the anger of the staff subsided. Gail was then able to say, "I understand what you are feeling. The kids really got to me today, too. But your job and my job is to help these kids grow. We can't give up on them or on ourselves. How can we support each other to avoid the power struggles, keep the kids on task, and make learning interesting? Let's figure out how to take this on one day at a time. Hopefully it will get easier, but don't expect that until enough of the kids buy into the program to help us."

Once their anger was acknowledged and accepted, staff members were ready to close ranks with the Director. Gail made it clear that her role was to support them to be skillful leaders. Their job was to win over fear-driven and anger-driven students to participate fully in what the school has to offer. Once a student gets to that point, no matter how far behind academically, then he or she will take the risks and make the investment necessary for learning. As Gail led them to refocus on the vision of the school, the staff were able to let go of their instinctive longing for help from the outside and to look for possibilities at hand within themselves and the students.

THE FLOC FOSTER HOME PROGRAM

One day a small group of FLOC staff and consultants was engaged in long range planning for our foster home program. Staff members were feeling overwhelmed by the unrelenting demands of clients for support and the courts for paperwork. They felt that all they did was put out fires. The job felt directionless and unsatisfying.

In this depressed state, we began to ask, "Who, really, is our primary client?" Is the primary client the child, the court, the birth parent, the foster parent, an adoptive parent, or the public agency that referred the child to FLOC and pays for foster care and family services? As we wrote the names of these various parties on newsprint, Eileen Mayers-Pasztor, a consultant from the Child Welfare League of America, took the marker and drew a circle around the child and the birth parent. "Here's the primary client," she said. "The client is the parent-child relationship. The goal of the system is to support this relationship, and when it breaks down, to enable the child to bond with a permanent substitute parent. This vision of the child in a stable, mutually bonded relationship with a caring adult is the driving force that will lead us beyond the chaos and the burnout we are experiencing. It's not the child or the parent but the parent-child relationship. The activities in this system need to align with supporting that relationship."

We sat in silence for a while. Ardrea Burrell, the program director, spoke for the group, "But that's not the way it is." Eileen responded, "You're right, and that's why you feel like you are running hard to stay in the same place. Our system isn't clear about its mission."

Under Ardrea's leadership, we began to ask ourselves how to get more mileage out of the enormous energy our staff was investing. We began to ask how we could get involved earlier with the birth mother—as she was making the decision to voluntarily place her child or children in foster care or as they were about to be taken from her. How might the city's child welfare system change from the remedial approach to the generative—

that is, from short term strategies of rescue and reducing immediate pain to alignment with the vision of intrinsically desirable outcomes?

Eileen shared an example of an experimental foster care program in England in which the foster parent, before she agreed to accept children, negotiated directly with the birth mother (and where possible, the father) about mutual responsibilities. The birth mother had to assume some specific regular responsibility, such as coming to the foster home and bathing her children three nights a week. The foster parent related to only one parent (or couple) at a time and only accepted that parent's child or children. In addition to caring for the children, the foster parent's role, in partnership with the agency social worker, was to support the bonding between children and parents and assist the parent(s) in addressing the issues or conditions that led to the child being placed in foster care. The social service agency paid the foster parent a living wage to do this.

The foster parent's objective was to keep the birth parent(s) involved in parenting responsibility and not let that responsibility get shifted over entirely to the state. If the birth mother was unable to parent the child on her own, she had to be willing to accept support toward resuming parenting, or else face the consequences that proceed from the breakdown— namely, termination of parental rights and placement of the child with an adoptive family.

The current welfare system is a creation of unconstrained rational assumptions. In the attempt to "solve" situations that place children at great risk, the government or its surrogate steps in and assumes parenting responsibility from the parent. The birth parent is allowed to retreat to a passive role. In this way accountability is shifted from the birth parent to the outside intervenor. This remedial process is not working. Children drift into foster care and from foster home to foster home without parental accountability. This is dehumanizing to the birth parent and the child, and sets up an exhausting job for social workers. As a contract agency in the city child welfare system, FLOC is caught in this process. We are looking for openings to spend more of our time and resources in preventive strategies than in the often futile task of trying to remediate long eroded parent-child relationships.

FLOC'S HOPE AND A HOME PROGRAM

Experience in another FLOC program brings out further distinctions between generative and remedial ways of thinking.

In the FLOC Hope and a Home program, we have had intense discussions about how to relate to homeless families. We agree that access to safe, decent shelter is essential for human beings to flourish. We also wonder how an organization with limited means can buy and then rent housing to families who might not take ownership of upkeep and maintenance of the property. The conservative argument exhorts caution: "You can't give people housing and expect them to appreciate it, value it, and be responsible. They have to earn something before they will value it." Liberals typically reply, "The issue is one of justice. Housing is a basic right. If we have it in our means to give, we must do so and live with the consequences."

There is a piece of truth in each argument. Conservatives are accurate in pointing to the connection between non-accountability and low self-esteem. And there is substance in the liberal view that generosity empowers change more than punishment. Both perceptions are essentially remedial—that is, they focus on the problem and who is to blame rather than a vision of an intrinsically desirable outcome. While valid, each insight by itself is too limited to work with the complex forces in this situation.

A generative stance provides a deeper perspective: offer an evolutionary process to be worked out step by step. Offer housing on a transition basis at an affordable price, then work out a partnership with the family to deal with repairs, upkeep, and regular payment of rent. Expect that renters will do their best, but that they will probably need support and accountability to meet that expectation.

Mike Young, director of FLOC's Hope and a Home program, aims to teach disorganized families responsibility for their own homes. Most families move into FLOC housing with long-standing feelings of powerlessness—an expectation that something beyond their control is going to happen to make them lose this place like they have lost others. They do not expect respect and prompt attention from the landlord. In the past, the landlord has been "the man," an impersonal figure whose interest is to collect the rent and hold down the costs of running the building. If tenants push him too hard on repairs, he will retaliate with higher rents. These families do not expect good service. In turn, they act out their disrespect for "the system" by poor housekeeping or by not reporting malfunctions until the damage is severe. With no relationship of mutual respect, they fall behind in the rent, then dig in to wait for eventual eviction, taking as much advantage as they can of the situation in the meantime.

Mike tries to change this scenario. He and his staff get to know every family personally and seek to enroll them as partners with FLOC in caring for the house. When something goes wrong, tenants are encouraged to call the office, and staff are trained to respond promptly. One staff responsibility is to teach the family to do minor repairs, and to bring in a professional when more is required.

Mike makes it clear that FLOC depends on prompt payment of rent, since it operates on a tight budget. Families are told to inform staff ahead of time if they are having trouble meeting the rent. Otherwise the rent is due on time, and if it is over a month late, eviction proceedings are started. Some of the families resist growth into accountability as much as the youths in the Learning Center. If they refuse to participate, we use the authority the city statute gives us to sue for eviction. But most of the families with a history of evictions develop, within a few months, a pattern of regular payment. Improved housekeeping follows improved morale and positive relationships with staff.

Housing is only one part of the process. When Mrs. Perkins and her six children moved from an emergency shelter into FLOC transitional housing, a host of problems surfaced. Mrs. Perkins was alcoholic. Her three teenage children ignored her efforts at family control, coming and going as they pleased. A younger child had a chronic health condition. Mrs. Perkins was overwhelmed to the point of almost complete apathy. Hope and a Home social worker Mary Jo Schumacher took on the task of supporting Mrs. Perkins in facing her circumstances, one piece at a time.

At first, Mrs. Perkins was too overwhelmed to take even simple steps alone. Mary Jo went with her to obtain health care and other city services, which involved hours in waiting rooms, dozens of forms, and treks from office to office. The investment paid off as Mrs. Perkins gradually took hold of her parenting responsibilities. After two years, she applied for a job. Now she is a civil service postal employee.

Having a manageable caseload enabled Mary Jo to work several times a week with Mrs. Perkins. Teaching and supporting Mrs. Perkins as she connected with public services was only a step in the larger developmental process of empowerment. The critical sign that empowerment was happening came when Mrs. Perkins began to experience her accountability for herself and her family as enlivening rather than oppressive. She began to assert herself in relationship to her teenage children. She experienced herself as both a strong and a caring parent. She wanted the family to get off welfare. She got a job, which presented new challenges to balance her responsibilities and keep some space for herself. This woman was empowered both by Mary Jo's support and by her own experience of success.

MANNA

Jim Dickerson and Kay Schultz were co-directors of Manna, a sister program to FLOC that buys, rehabs, and sells housing to low- and moderate-income families. Before creating Manna, Jim directed the FLOC Hope and a Home program. In his former role, he envisioned a continuum of housing services being offered to homeless families and poor families living in overcrowded conditions. At one end he saw short-term emergency shelter that could hold families together after they were evicted or lost their housing because of rent hikes, fire, or loss of a job. Short-term intervention could give family and staff time to assess needs, work out a plan, and strengthen the family. Next on the continuum, he saw transitional housing— housing for several months to two or three years. Rent would be subsidized and families would agree to work with staff in a goal-setting process to achieve stability and move to independence.

At the far end of the continuum, Jim saw the need for permanent housing for low income families. Condominium conversions have drastically reduced available rental housing, and state and federal housing initiatives have virtually halted. Jim met some developers, small and large, who bought condemned housing at public auctions and thought his group could find houses there too. How much money would it take to get some of these houses and small apartment buildings, rehab them, and sell them to low income families? Where would the financing come from? Where could he find carpenters and plumbers and foremen who would work for what Manna could pay?

Assessing the need, the obstacles, and the possible partners pushed Jim toward inventing his vision. For several years, Jim went every week to spend a day in retreat in a nearby Catholic monastery. In the solitude, he held together in his mind the crying need and the myriad obstacles alongside the question, "Setting the issue of resources aside, what do I and others want for our city in the area of housing?"

Gradually a vision emerged from this internal dialogue. Jim saw many diverse city and suburban partners collaborating to offer a dynamic continuum of housing and support services, enabling low-income District of Columbia families to significantly improve their lives, stabilize and develop their neighborhoods, and serve others in the process.

Jim shared this vision with Kay Schultz, who had worked with low income housing cooperatives. Kay brought both knowledge and technical skill in putting together housing deals with government and commercial investors. Jim brought an intuitive ability to spot workable deals and partners, and the charisma and communication skills to bring diverse people together. Jim and Kay became a powerful team. Soon others responded, and within five years the program was adding between 60 and 80 rehabilitated units to the low income home ownership market every year.

This process started when one person created a new institution in his mind and enrolled others in commitment to the vision. Jim and Kay are leaders who orchestrate people to confront the unworkability of both an exclusively profit-driven housing system and the public housing system as presently designed. They invite others to align their diverse positions with a vision of sharing the risks of converting run-down housing into affordable housing at the lowest possible costs. Within this framework of shared risk in addressing a critical social need, it becomes possible for actors as different as realtors, bankers, and social activists to pool their resources and experiment their way toward a common goal.

WHAT POOR PEOPLE WANT

The generative orientation presses the question: "What do people really want?" This is the starting place for shaping a compelling vision that projects the kind of society we are looking for.

When comfortable Americans make assumptions about what the poor want, they generally operate out of the dominant remedial orientation. They correctly assume that the poor want to stop hurting, but because of their narrow assumptions, they fail to acknowledge the driving force of aspiration in all people, the poor as well as the comfortable.

Pain is easily understood when it is physical. But it is also psychological and spiritual. Pain exists whenever there is acute discrepancy between what we hold to be intrinsically worthwhile and the actual living of our lives. Embedded in the immediate experience of pain is a permanent tension which Abraham Maslow describes as a hierarchy of human needs. At bottom is the need for physical survival, which requires a critical minimum of food, clothing, and shelter. When that need is met, the need for physical and psychological safety emerges as a dominant drive. As safety needs are met, consciousness is directed toward the need for belonging, and then toward a sense of self or identity. As a sense of self gets stronger, one confronts the need to be creative, to make a difference, to self-actualize (to be all that one can be).

The following is Maslow's famous diagram:

THE EVOLUTIONARY TENSION
OF HUMAN WANTS

Instead of asking, "What do African Americans (or women or the poor or any other marginalized group) want?," we may assume all human beings have the same basic needs and that these needs figure into whatever drives the evolution of civilization. Pain occurs whenever persons and groups are stuck or stymied in their ability to meet fundamental needs and to expand into higher dimensions of need satisfaction. From this perspective, the boredom of those who have enough and don't know what to do with their lives is as real, albeit not as obvious as the hunger pains of those who go all day without food. The physical pain of a blow to the body, or cancer, is unavoidably recognized. What often goes unnoticed is the longing for the experience of belonging, self-identity, and making a contribution.

Human dignity is rooted in the ontological fact that aspiration is universally human. It isn't created. It doesn't disappear. Aspiration simply is. No matter how mired in economic degradation or psychological numbness, no child or adult on God's earth totally loses the capacity to aspire. The one exception may be the psychopath or sociopath who has lost all connection with human feeling and value.

What do the poor want? What do the comfortable want? What do third world and first world countries want? Experience tells us that if we are really hungry and cold, our consciousness will normally be dominated by the need for food, clothing, and shelter. And before we can risk expressing who we are in the face of possible disapproval (gain self-identity), we must have acquired through experience a basic trust in our continuing physical and psychological safety. Likewise, while an economic goal, such as owning a car, a house, or a pair of Air Jordan basketball shoes, may seem overly materialistic to a person engaged in the drive for self-actualization, these material goals are critical transitions for people who are moving from preoccupation with basic safety to the next level, which is experiencing belonging.

Linda Brown's story illustrates the relationship of behavior to consciousness. Linda, a middle-aged African American woman with three children, contacted the FLOC Hope and a Home program when she was facing eviction from a doubled-up housing situation. Linda had lethargically shifted from one entry-level job to another, and from apartment to apartment, often sharing quarters with another family to manage the rent. Her basic assumption was that life would always be this way, and the best she could look forward to was to ensure that she and her children survived and were as safe as possible in the high crime areas where she could afford housing. FLOC rented her a house at an affordable rent on a safe street and helped her furnish it.

At first she thought she had arrived, but then she knew she hadn't. FLOC owned the house, and the deal was that within three years she would move on to get housing on her own so that FLOC could rent to another family living in the shelter system or in doubled-up housing. Hope and a Home director Mike Young told Linda about the Manna program and the possibility of buying her own home through Manna. He invited her to join the Homebuyers' Club that he and Manna co-director Kay Schultz had started. Linda hesitantly joined, still doubting that her life would ever be different.

At Homebuyers' Club meetings, Linda was part of a peer group where she and other poor people talked about ways to purchase housing and the responsibilities of home ownership. After about a year of regular participation Linda was hooked. One night she took her credit card and thought "the only way I can see myself saving enough to own a house is to pay as I go." She took out her scissors and cut up her credit card. That symbolic act was like jumping a chasm. Later, she told a friend that before she made up her mind for home ownership, she had lived her life half asleep. The decision to "go for it" woke her up. Linda succeeded in buying a three-bedroom, completely restored Manna house, after putting down $500 in carefully protected savings and committing herself to a 30-year mortgage at the same rate she had been accustomed to pay for rent. Later Linda joined the Hope and a Home staff as housing counselor.

In Chapter Nine, I raised the question: how do we get there from here?—"there" being a civilization that supports humanity in flourishing, and "here" being a society that supports the comfortable in acquiring possessions and supports the poor in dependency. This vision calls us both to see the limitations of the existing political debate and to widen that debate by a generative way of thinking. In the next chapter, we will explore the contrast between remedial and generative ways of thinking in relation to illegal drugs.

Chapter Eleven

A DIFFERENT TAKE ON THE DRUG CRISIS

In the introduction to this book, I described the Kerner Commission's assessment that the U.S. is headed in the direction of two separate countries with no economic, social, or spiritual identification with each other—one predominantly white and comfortable, and the other predominantly black and poor. The drift toward "two Americas" reinforces the entrenchment of poverty, and the condition of poverty is supporting the drug epidemic. Both are seriously undermining the future of this country.

In this chapter we will explore how this drift toward two Americas supports the extension of persistent poverty and drugs, then illustrate how the existing liberal-conservative political debate mis-states the issues, and how the generative orientation speaks with greater relevance and power.

In Chapter Nine, I described two competing political orientations, the remedial and the generative. I submit that they evoke opposite responses to social conditions such as drugs and poverty. The remedial orientation engages social conditions in terms of what is not working. It seeks to analyze the causative forces, and then sets goals to contain these forces (conservative) or change them (liberal).

The generative orientation, on the other hand, looks at the world bi-focally. One focus acknowledges existing conditions. The other focus visualizes a new arrangement based on what is intrinsically worthwhile to the people immersed in the conditions, and to the viewer. With a generative orientation, one switches back and forth between current reality (immediate conditions) and distant vision (desired result) until one can almost see the two simultaneously—but without merging one into the other. This is a critical distinction. The generative orientation is not utopian in a traditional sense, but steers one through a constant dialectic between current conditions and intrinsically desirable possibilities.

The driving force of the remedial orientation is fear of the problem's spread (conservative) or anger at its existence (liberal). In contrast, the driving force of the generative orientation is love for the envisioned new arrangement. These distinctly different driving forces set up different processes and evoke different energies. Fear is basically defensive and protective. Anger implies blame and the stance of superior goodness or innocence on the part of the blamer. It increases the distance between blamer and blamed, and reduces access between them.

Love, on the other hand, is open, outreaching. It invites exchange and participation. It creates a climate that makes it safe to risk, to fail as well as to succeed. Love supports the growth of trust and self-esteem, and it releases energy to engage in expansive evolutionary growth on the part of both giver and receiver. The current climate for engaging the society-wide issues of drugs and poverty is dominated by fear and anger. The generative orientation offers a way to shift to the far more dynamic force of love.

DRUGS AND A DIVIDED AMERICAN SOCIETY

It is ironic indeed that comfortable America, which largely excludes poor America from legitimate trade, political influence, and cultural exchange, colludes with it to feed the parasitic drug industry. Without the investment of surplus wealth from the middle and upper classes, drug trafficking in this country would be a minor social problem. The drug problem is driven by the demand of large numbers of middle and upper class whites and blacks who are willing to use much, in some cases all, of their discretionary income to obtain drugs. They are also willing to do business with total strangers at floating open-air markets, and to pay cash with no questions asked. In short, they sanction and support drug trafficking while avoiding identification with it.

The illegal drug industry is underground, and heavily staffed at the street level with poor black youths. Black children as young as eight years of age are recruited to work, first as lookouts, then as "holders" of "stash" for dealers. From there it is a short step to become dealers themselves at the age when other youths are getting their first paying jobs. These poor youths become entrepreneurs in a clever, gigantic, clandestine business which compensates them with wages and commissions, producing a level of disposable income exceeding that of the richest children in America. Neighborhood drug dealers pay children generously to "hold their stash." Unless the police catch dealers with the drugs on them, no charge will hold up in court. The shift from helper to dealer is extremely seductive for a poor and unsupervised adolescent. It appears to be a way, perhaps the only way, to rise above survival to freedom, respect, identity, acquisition. It is not uncommon for inner city residents to observe youngsters counting wads of $1000 or more.

The illegal drug industry is cleverly embedded in the highly effective and largely hidden infrastructure of an international marketing and supply network, protected and abetted by foreign dictators, organized crime, and highly placed accomplices, and nestled in the bosom of the military-industrial complex. The front-end sales people take the personal risks necessary to market the product on the street in exchange for immediate, lucrative pay-offs. So it is that the poor are cut in on the deal to live high for a short time, against heavy odds of ending in jail or dead.

The conditions that surround the children of drug-involved parents are almost unbelievable. In Washington, DC, social workers estimate that 60% to 80% of their child protective services caseload is comprised of families involved with drugs. In many cases, the mother uses drugs and pays with income from prostitution or selling drugs, or she lets her home be used for drug sales by male friends. These mothers go in and out of a catatonic stupor, leaving their children to raise themselves. One social worker recently testified about a home visit with a drug addicted mother and a two-year-old child. The mother was so lethargic from her drug hangover that she passively and uncomprehendingly watched her child help herself to a drink of water dipped out of the toilet. Even more appalling are the cases of infants born with small brains and missing body parts because their mothers used crack cocaine during pregnancy.

Youths involved in the drug business present us with a very mixed picture. They are not pitiful. They have the strengths that entrepreneurial drug activity calls forth. Nor are they altogether deluded. These youths are setting goals and managing their options very assertively, and will continue to do so in their own limited context. They see the larger society ignoring their needs, and they choose from the options immediately at hand. Rather than die a slow death of despair in the virtually impossible task of catching up with educated blacks and whites in legitimate pursuits, they are choosing a go at the fast lane. And they are not necessarily driven by greed. In fact, some of the youngsters who choose the drug business display "higher qualities," such as generosity and loyalty. Along with buying snappy necklaces, shoes, clothes, and automobiles for themselves, they support their families, pay rent, and buy expensive gifts for their loved ones, including cars, homes, and stylish clothes—the same things comfortable

Americans value. Beneath their choice of drug dealing is a positive evolutionary force—namely, the aspiration to participate in a higher quality of life. These youths watch television. They watch what goes on in the streets. They observe who gets "respect." They make the connection between attention-getting possessions like gold necklaces, expensive clothes, fancy cars, and respect. Unfortunately, their concept of quality of life turns back upon itself, putting them in a box rather than on an open-ended way to a larger existence.

DISCERNING THE UNDERLYING FORCES

Generative thinking assumes that within *all* conditions, evolutionary forces of aspiration are present, which, if acknowledged and worked with, are strong enough to ultimately realize those aspirations. The generative orientation also assumes that because life is always evolving, the breakdown of old structures and patterns is inevitable. When old systems reach and exceed their limits and break down, demand for what is new surfaces.

From a generative perspective, drugs represent the limit and the breakdown of an old social order needing to evolve. The old order is no longer adequate to realize the aspirations of the evolving society, and holds people captive in a situation where the costs of surviving exceed the benefits and satisfactions. This deficit creates frustration. And the greater the discrepancy between the investment of one's life spirit and the benefits of that investment, the greater the frustration. When frustration gets high enough, one must either move into a higher level of participation in life or find an outlet to compensate for or anesthetize the frustration of being stuck at a low level.

The incredible spread of alcohol and other drug dependency points to an old social order reaching its limit and beginning to break down. This is a social order that makes acquisition of wealth its dominant value. Generative thinking acknowledges that the drive to acquire wealth is in itself a positive force. Civilizations have evolved by families forming into tribes and tribes into countries. Stabilization as tribes, communities, and nations then permitted the specialization of individuals in ways that led to innovation, which in turn benefited everyone. Specialization in terms of skills, services, and products generated exchange, and therefore acquisition. Moreover, with regard to human development, acquisition is critical for helping individuals to develop an independent identity and gain status. And the evolution of processes for acquisition by exchange rather than plunder leads to general economic and cultural expansion.

But an attachment to acquisition as the single, dominant value leads to diminishment. For example, in this country we expect that with material success will come security and general well-being. But a large percentage of well-off Americans remain insecure even though they have a comfortable life style with assets and reserves. When insecurity as an undefinable and insatiable need drives our acquisitiveness, then no matter how much we acquire, it is never enough. People who get on this treadmill often don't know how to get off.

Thus the appeal of drugs for the middle and upper classes. Using drugs can buy a "high" that one's life is not providing, or can deaden the misery of emptiness. Emptiness yawns when one invests more and more of one's life energy in acquisition, only to note declining returns in terms of satisfaction. Drugs deaden the pain, but they also deaden the person's awareness of possibilities for an expanded life that deserve attention.

For the poor also, drugs offer immediate experience, a pleasurable intensity which does not seem available otherwise. And selling drugs is so lucrative that it provides immediate access to what the majority culture seems to value as the "good life." Practically anyone willing to take the risk can get in on the action.

At bottom the drug epidemic is driven by a positive force—its "evolutionary intent."[1] Evolutionary intent is the inherent drive of the human species to evolve to a more expansive life. For comfortable America this means a shift from a social order based narrowly on acquiring products and possessions to a social and economic order oriented to the expansion of experience (self-enrichment, travel, intimacy, personal creativity, and so on). For some, expanded life would be creative life. Creative life is living in congruence with our highest aspirations for both the world and ourselves. The person participating in life at this level gets the kind of satisfaction out of creative effort toward his or her highest aspirations that a poor youth gets out of acquiring possessions that attract "respect."

For the poor, the need is for first-time inclusion in the acquisitional economy. For the poor to evolve, the comfortable must evolve, and in the process create new service demands that provide economic incentives to the poor. Consider the possibilities if only a portion of the enormous sums of money now spent on alcohol and other drug use, advertising of legal drugs, alcohol and drug treatment, policing, and adjudication were redirected to non-chemical expansion of experience.

We cannot deal with the drug culture or the poverty culture in our schools and our streets simply by promoting discipline, threatening punishment, or promising solutions. The only strategies that will matter over the long term are those that tap into and uncover the numbed aspirations of youths who see no future for themselves in this society. We need a "use economy" that enables people to use resources without having to own them. This can lead to abundance in the form of abundant use, abundant experience, and abundant participation. The use of wealth is not limited by shortage of resources, but acquisition must be in service to experience and activity, not unmet security needs. Egalitarian distribution, championed by liberals, is too static to achieve abundance. It is rooted in the old acquisition-based social order that equates abundance with possessions.

"SOLUTIONS" WE HAVE TRIED

Persistent poverty in the United States today can be traced to the institution of slavery and the subsequent sharecrop system of farming in the South. These systems represent failure to evolve with consequences extending into the present. The institution of slavery was in the process of breaking down even before the Civil War. Production could not offset the economic and moral cost of maintaining slavery. Rather than deal with the negative cost-benefit reality of slavery, and get on with its next stage of evolution, the South started a war, exhausted its resources, and then tried to make do with a sharecrop-based agricultural system that was almost as regressive as the institution of slavery. This affected both freed slaves and landless whites. Both groups, along with the entire region, were excluded from the evolution to an industrial economy that was taking place in the larger society.

The federal Freedman's Bureau established for numbers of freed slaves what Bayard Rustin called "stairsteps out of poverty." Many blacks made their way into business and the professions. Many other freed slaves and poor whites, however, were trapped in the economic decline of the post-Civil War South with no stairsteps in sight. Many of their descendants, white and black, are the people most dependent upon government social service programs and transfer payments.

Government remedial strategies since Roosevelt have had a very mixed effect. Some people used various government aid programs for assistance until they could manage on their own. But others were caught in processes of disempowerment. When the jobs created by improving economic conditions were denied them because of racism or lack of education, they were stuck on the dole. To the compliant, it seemed natural that responsibility for their well-being should reside with those same government programs. Over time, even the programs themselves accepted this shift of responsibility. Even when the administrators of social programs began to talk about "helping people help themselves," the structure and processes of the social service delivery system supported the transfer of accountability from recipient to intervenor.

Recently, we as a country have pursued two strategies in the attempt to "solve" drugs and persistent poverty. It is significant that we have framed both under the rubric of war: the 1960s War on Poverty and the current "War on Drugs."

The 1960s War on Poverty drew on unconstrained rational assumptions that poverty, like any other human problem, can be rationally diagnosed and a solution planned and implemented. The basic diagnosis was that poverty results from economic and social inequality. The remedy was to eliminate the causes by a redistribution of wealth, eradicate racial discrimination by governmental fiat, and overcome the effects of prior deprivation through remediation programs.

The unconstrained rational paradigm attempts, through taxation, to top off the incentive to acquire and to redirect this wealth toward filling in the bottom of the economic curve. In the War on Poverty this strategy made a temporary difference. During the period from 1960 to 1980, the American economy expanded to absorb 50 million new workers, of whom a large percentage were women and offspring of the postwar "baby boom." While the private sector economy absorbed these new workers, the public sector, through various government programs, cut the poverty rate from 19% in 1965 to 9% in 1972.[2] The unconstrained rational strategy on poverty, however, eventually stalled because its demand for ever-increasing funds came up against a range of other demands, from pollution control to the Vietnam War to the expansion of government regulations. Meanwhile, the isolation of the persistently poor not only continued but intensified in the tug-of-war between liberal and conservative assumptions.

Whereas the war on poverty was based on unconstrained rational or liberal assumptions, the current war on drugs represents the constrained rational or conservative paradigm. Both are remedial in orientation, and are in fact wars. One fights human nature (the war on drugs), and the other fought a problem held to be structural (war on poverty). Thus far the war on drugs is using two principal strategies: first, law and order, aimed at apprehending violators, and secondly, education, aimed at potential drug users ("Just say no"). Both strategies aim at containment by fear.

NEEDED: AN EVOLUTIONARY LEAP

It is the absence of any clear sense of moving toward something that makes both conservative and liberal arguments about poverty and drugs unconvincing. Neither argument is compelling because neither deals with human aspiration. The "solutions" are heavily dependent upon outside intervention in the form of law enforcement or top-down social programs. The solutions don't get down to the real issue, so they each generate negative side effects that exceed their benefits. *The real issue is resistance to evolution by the comfortable and exclusion of the poor from the possibility of evolution.* It is time for an evolutionary leap beyond the existing debate to a new orientation and a corresponding new set of assumptions.

A generative orientation toward drugs would acknowledge its evolutionary intent—expanded life. A wise priest said this in religious terms: "Alcoholism is a thirst for God." It is the cry of a lonely soul for a relationship of deep acceptance. The founder of Alcoholics Anonymous saw this and gave it form in the 12 step program. In brief, recovery is based upon a vision of expanded life and sticking with the program to get there with the support of fellow strugglers.

What about poverty? What could be an evolutionary intent within this monstrosity? I recently visited Singapore, which has virtually eliminated poverty over the last 10 years through economic policies aimed dually at economic growth and inclusion of the entire population in that growth, not by welfare but political decisions aimed at giving everyone an economic stake in the country. The years of deprivation dating from colonial days through Japanese occupation during World War II prepared the ground for a sea change of economic and political thinking directed toward universal housing, quality education and health care, and full employment. While we Americans are justifiably critical of the autocratic process in Singapore for achieving economic inclusion, their success in working with evolutionary forces for the common good is instructive.

To realize the evolutionary intent of drugs, poverty, pollution, the starvation of our artistic consciousness, racism, sexism, and other ills, we need a new social goal, based on a new vision. This vision must project quality of life, not just quantity of possessions; this vision must evoke participation by all, in both opportunity and responsibility. A generative social goal would make room for economic as well as developmental diversity, and would move toward high-level participation in life for all.

A new social goal would describe where we are trying to go—to a state of health and flourishing—and not merely the absence of problems like crime, drugs, and poverty. Our shared sense of what social wellness might be, even though we have yet to experience it, would serve as a focus to the commitment to align efforts beyond the narrow concerns of any group's special interests and boundaries. To get a compelling picture of social wellness, I refer the reader to the diagram of liberating circles that lead to liveliness, initiative and safety, on page 75 in Chapter Four.

RISKTAKING: A GENERATIVE ESSENTIAL

My educator friend Joe McCaleb believes that learning involves risk. "Not many of our children are taking risks," he says. "They move along like they're on a conveyor belt in a factory, with frequent squirts of information thrust at them and little leadership for risk taking. No wonder drugs are so inviting to the young."

Like the issue of education, the issues of poverty and drugs are not simply about more opportunity or more discipline. They are deeply rooted societal conditions that require transformation, not remediation. The issue is transformation from lower stages of life experience to higher stages. This involves both leadership in seizing opportunities for transformation and risk taking on the part of the individual and society.

Another example. Nancy Van Scoyoc, former director of the FLOC Outdoor Education Center, decided that she wanted to do something to respond to the needs of children in shelters for the homeless in the District of Columbia. She conceived of a three-week wilderness summer school for a dozen boys aged 10-14, then living in shelters. The goal was to challenge these boys to do some academic risk-taking in the relaxing setting of the out of doors. She recruited a small staff of men with both classroom and outdoor experiential education training.

The first week of the camp was very frustrating. The kids felt to the staff like dead weight. They were unresponsive to what staff members had thought would be stimulating learning opportunities—doing math with physical materials and games; high interest, easy-to-read books; a ropes course to encourage teamwork; swimming and canoeing. Instead of responding, the boys immediately fell into their accustomed patterns of provoking fistfights and teasing anyone who seemed halfway involved.

The staff was on the verge of despair when the sighting of a rattlesnake provided a unique teachable moment. Students and teachers gathered around the coiled snake. One boy wanted to kill it, but the teacher stopped him with the question, "What is the benefit of having this snake alive?" The boys listened, thought, and risked responses. Then two kids volunteered to read up on rattlesnakes in the camp encyclopedia and report to the group at lunch. These boys had never used an encyclopedia before.

That was the turning point toward the transformation of the last 10 days of camp. Real learning began. It became contagious. When parents and siblings came out on the last day, the boys showed the small dam they had built, the 20-foot collage they had created, and the books they had read. They didn't want to go home; instead they wanted their families to move out there. The first thing 14-year-old Kendrick did upon his return to the Capital City Inn emergency shelter was to go to the neighborhood library, get a card, and check out four books. His mother called Nancy the following day in disbelief, "What did you do with my son?"

I happened to be giving the sermon the next day in my church. I used the occasion to tell about the camp and the boys, and asked for volunteers to pair with the families as supporting friends. Ten people volunteered, and under Nancy's direction we began a people-to-people follow-up. The issue was the same— risk taking: for the parents to take steps toward getting housing, and for the volunteers to expose themselves to the risks of a personal relationship with a homeless family.

Two years later, Kendrick agreed to tell his story about life in the shelter system to a Senate hearing on homelessness chaired by Senator Paul Simon. He answered a series of thoughtful questions from the Senator with a poise far beyond his years.

The point of this example is not primarily the need for opportunity, although that is extremely important. These boys knew what an encyclopedia was. They had seen them on school bookshelves, and Kendrick knew the location of the public library and how to get a card. These opportunities had been there all along. The difference was an event that called Kendrick and the other boys to risk themselves in engaging with opportunity. In many cases the obstacle is not lack of resources but lack of commitment. And commitment is often linked to leadership.

THE CRUCIAL ROLE OF LEADERSHIP

Barbara McGhee, a mother of three who participated for a time in the FLOC Hope and a Home program, gave me this poem she had written, entitled "The Cry of the Children."

> Can't you hear the children of the world
>   crying out to us,
> Something is wrong, something is missing
>   from our lives,
> Something the young people of yesterday had.
> They don't know exactly what it is,
> Yet they feel this void.
> Don't you hear them screaming out to us?
> They walk the streets searching for it,
> Whatever it is that is missing.
> What is the answer to their cry?
> Is it us, this new breed of society?
> Or is it just that times have changed?
> No matter what, there has to be an answer soon.

The boys on that FLOC summer camp got a taste of abundance, and they liked it. Even though there was absolutely no difference in their bank accounts, they engaged in the experience of abundance—with the forest, with the rustic dining hall and tents, with food, in their new relationships with one another and the adults who led them. Two years later half of this same group returned for another camp experience. This time they were ready to assert their own leadership. They started camp by setting goals. One goal was to keep the peace—no fighting. Another was to complete a four-day backpacking trip, using a compass to plot the course. A third was to build a cabin for their own use and use by others. This year the boys were able to find excitement on their own.

In hindsight, the rattlesnake incident had presented the opportunity for an evolutionary leap. The boys responded. It was a small jump—the risk of participation. What the FLOC staff and program did was to help them shift to a new level of awareness, and then offer a series of opportunities that deepened their new awareness until it became natural. Then they could not go back. They would regress from time to time, but they wouldn't go back to being unaware.

In the generative orientation, leadership is not only about getting things done, but, more fundamentally, about discerning and seizing pregnant opportunities to lead people into expanded awareness. Then the expanded awareness becomes a driving force for spontaneous action and growth. Commitment is not so much about overcoming forces of inertia as it is about engaging forces of aspiration. The higher our level of participation, the higher our energy. Energy is self-renewing when we are engaged in effort that connects with our aspiration, when we have moved past ambivalence to commitment.

BEYOND RATIONALITY

The generative orientation takes us beyond rationality. This does not mean ignoring reason or going back to prerational emotional scripts. Evolutionary intent is never as simple as reversing the situation—making someone drug-free instead of addicted, comfortable instead of poor. Evolutionary intent points us toward aspirations we have not acknowledged before and structures we have not experienced before. These realities do not exist within our current frame of reference. *With regard to poverty and drugs, our goal is not to rescue people, not even the children.*

Our goal is to develop strong, autonomous, risk-taking people—both children and adults. If we only attack current demons like drugs and persistent poverty, we may get what we asked for and find that it is something worse—like a police state or a uniform mediocrity without incentives. We can do better. The way to begin is to generate a compelling vision for our community, nation, and world and then experiment our way toward its realization.

We will never figure out one ideal system to combat child abuse, drugs, teen pregnancy, unemployment, school drop-outs, and so on. We will never be able to plan a program that won't need to evolve or be experimented with. In fact, we may do better to skip tampering with the present system and go straight to catalyzing worthwhile experiments that align with the eventual outcome we are seeking. Ultimately, if we are generative in our orientation, that

CHAPTER ELEVEN

outcome will be about abundance—abundant use, abundant experience, abundant participation.

A generative orientation assumes that a single individual, an organization, a political party, and even a country can work with underlying forces by allowing aspirations, rather than remedies, to define the way we see the problem. The starting point for progress is to acknowledge that we cannot change the forces at play in human affairs. We don't need to. We can work with these forces by grasping their evolutionary intent.

Chapter Twelve

CHOOSING A FUTURE THAT
WORKS FOR EVERYONE

We as a nation are now in a position where we either move boldly forward to include those who have been left behind, or we settle for freedom for the comfortable and containment of the rest. Drifting with the status quo moves us deeper and deeper into containment. A future of containment of the left-out—more police, jails, public feeding stations for the hungry, shelters for the homeless, large orphanages for abandoned children, repressive schools— is prohibitively costly in the long run.

A future of inclusion, while requiring more effort, is far more enlivening in every way, morally, spiritually, and economically. In the latter case, every poor child who becomes a successful parent, wage earner, and contributing citizen represents a major transfer from the debit column of containment to the credit column of inclusion. How can we get to a future of inclusion? The place to start is where we are. What we need is a broad movement of diverse stakeholders taking our direction from a compelling vision of inclusion, scaling down that vision into practical projects, and going into action where we are.

FLOC FUTURE SEARCH CONFERENCE

In March, 1994, more than 60 people gathered at For Love of Children for a three-day conference to generate a shared vision for Washington, DC children and families in the year 2004 and FLOC's role in contributing to the realization of that vision. The conference brought together a rich cross-section of stakeholders—neighborhood residents; a judge; a school board member; representatives of other private and public agencies; representatives of business and labor; youth; parents; arts groups; FLOC board members, staff at every level, clients, and volunteers. Two-thirds of the group were directly connected with FLOC; one-third were from outside constituent groups. The idea was to get the whole system—in this case the child welfare system—into the room; generate massive information about the past, present trends, and possible futures; and then narrow our information and efforts into do-able projects.

A "Future Search Conference" is a new planning technology, a fast-paced process for generating broad information and perspectives, then inventing a shared vision of the future that is rooted in the aspirations and commitment of the diverse stakeholders. It is designed as a "mind blowing" experience, to break out of old conceptual boxes and position participants to think freely and imaginatively about a desired future.

We first brainstormed about changes in the FLOC organization, the city, and the world over the last three decades, inviting participants to record their input on a 50-foot sheet of newsprint taped on the walls. We noted the start of the Peace Corps, the assassinations of John and Robert Kennedy and Martin Luther King, Jr., the Civil Rights Movement, the War on Poverty, the Hippie generation, the sexual revolution, landing on the moon, etc., etc. Individuals marked marriages, divorces, births, deaths, major changes in their lives. Organizationally, we noted the start of FLOC, the closing of Junior Village, the opening and closing of the child advocacy center, and the restructuring of FLOC's year-round wilderness school into a summer and weekend youth training program.

When we got to current trends we noted the new possibilities offered by the computer, shifts in thinking about organizational change, community development, the potential of reinventing government, and public-private partnerships that redistribute responsibility and accountability. As we looked at current trends in our city, frustration quickly surfaced. Enormous human potential is being lost. Violence is spreading. Major shifts in the economy have removed the bottom rungs from the fabled American ladder of opportunity. Instead of safety in their schools and neighborhoods, inner city children face physical danger; instead of economic security, families face uncertainty; instead of intellectual stimulation, children face boredom and stagnation; in place of respect, youths see themselves ignored and rejected. Lacking clear and consistent adult expectations, many youths feel deeply alienated from mainstream American society.

Then we started creating images of a desired future for our city and its children and families ten years ahead, working by tables of eight, and creating role plays to share with the other participants. The conference facilitators, Jackie McMakin, Susan Gardner, and Joachim Willis, recorded the main themes that emerged from the role plays. We voted with little stickers for those we considered most important. Out of this we generated the following vision:

- a city of thriving neighborhoods in which every child and every family is known and valued;

- where neighborhood-accountable education/ service centers are equipping neighborhood children, youth, and parents to take over responsibility for their own self-development through training, trustful relationships, and exposure to new possibilities;

- where traditional service models which assume that something is wrong with the client and in which service moves one way from service provider to client are replaced by two-way models that embody coaching, exchange, and teamwork.

The final task was to scale down this broad

vision into potential projects that the FLOC organization with the support of its external stakeholders could conceptualize and implement. Four major emphases were identified:

- developing a holistic, comprehensive neighborhood-based family support center in the inner city Shaw community where FLOC is based;

- pioneering educational methods and technologies that empower children, youths, and parents to recognize and build on their strengths and transcend their self-imposed/culture-imposed limits;

- joining forces with others to create a powerful grassroots advocacy voice for children, families, and neighborhoods with the general public, the City Council, and Congress;

- using computer technology to increase community access to information about available resources, streamline paperwork and track outcomes, and expose children and parents to computer training, thus expanding their job possibilities.

SHARING WITH POTENTIAL STAKEHOLDERS

No one owns a vision. No one has proprietary rights. The nature of vision is that it belongs to whomever identifies with it. A vision exists to be shared and to enroll stakeholders who work toward the vision, either independently or collaboratively. Either way there is gain. That is the power of vision.

As this is being written it is too early to tell how the momentum created by the FLOC Future Search Conference will play out. It may be helpful, however, to describe how the vision is assuming a life of its own in the midst of a changing environment. This is an example of the generative process in action.

An immediate question is: What will happen to the District of Columbia child welfare system as a whole, which is at present a government-run system assisted by nonprofit and for profit contracting agencies? This question is being asked in the midst of the city's worse fiscal crisis in over 100 years. An annual deficit exceeding 25% of the city's annual budget is forcing the city government to downsize and cut programs. Meanwhile, child abuse and neglect has risen over 25 percent in the past year. Some are even calling for orphanages again in spite of the prohibitive costs of institutional care financially and to children.

Some years ago I attended a week-long IBM training conference given as a public service for not-for-profit agency leaders. The conference focused on the situation we are now facing, of mounting social problems and shrinking government resources. What do you do when you have to do more with less? IBM's answer was:

You look for *breakthrough solutions.* I was intrigued then and find the approach even more compelling today.

In order to see breakthrough solutions you first have to get out of your mental boxes left over from the past. We discussed this in Chapter Nine in connection with paradigm shifts. A paradigm operates as a filter to let in or screen out ideas and possibilities. It is based on the beliefs and rules of the individual, organization, or system.

Shortly after the Future Search Conference, public child welfare agency middle managers approached the Consortium on Child Welfare, an 18-member group of D.C. nonprofit foster care, adoption, and family service providers, of which FLOC is a founding member, with a request that we develop more foster homes to meet the mounting need. Their request created the opportunity for starting a new conversation.

Yes, we were interested in helping. At the same time, we were convinced that if we kept doing foster care the same old way, we would keep getting the same result—an ever expanding system and no prospects for getting ahead of the curve. We asked them to consider a different strategy—namely, combining foster home recruitment with the development of family support services in the same neighborhoods. The goal would be to build capacity at the neighborhood level, both to prevent family breakup and to provide foster care when necessary, which limits disruption in the children's lives and supports the continuity of same school, friends, extended family assistance, etc. In essence, we were asking the public agency to collaborate with us in testing a new paradigm—essentially an *organic paradigm* of growing community capacity.

PARADIGM SHIFT:
FROM RESCUE TO CAPACITY-BUILDING

What we want to do is test the feasibility of a new way of doing services that stems from two critical distinctions. First is the distinction between social services as a *rescue strategy* and as a *capacity-building strategy*. Social services in the District of Columbia and most other cities are currently structured on a traditional rescue model. We are proposing a reconfiguration of philosophy and structure that would lead to a capacity-building model.

Both rescue and capacity-building strategies are needed. A three-year-old child wandering unattended on the street and people caught in a burning building need to be rescued. We need agencies like child protective services and the fire department with the authority and capacity to act when the need arises. The system breaks down, however, when a rescue strategy becomes the single strategy that consumes all of the available public and private funding to the neglect of preventive strategies and community capacity-building.

Rescuing becomes a problem when you interfere with people's power or a community's power by doing something for them that they can and ought to do for themselves. By operating as a closed system and taking over total responsibility, public agencies deny the family and the community the opportunity to be effective and to learn from experience. When you rescue in this way, you actually devalue and disempower the person or community. Because social welfare policy and practice in this country have failed to evolve, most economically devastated neighborhoods are now environments of service where the industrial-era ladder of opportunity has been taken away. Residents come to believe that their survival and well-being depend upon being a client. They see themselves as people and neighborhoods with special needs and deficits to be met by outsiders, and gradually become mainly consumers of services with no incentive to be producers. Consumers of services focus vast amounts of creativity and intelligence on the survival challenge of outwitting the system, or on finding ways—in the formal or illegal economy—to bypass the system.[1]

THE SIGNIFICANCE OF INFRASTRUCTURE

A second distinction we want to develop is the concept of *infrastructure*. Infrastructures can be either formal or informal. Formal infrastructures are institutional systems like the foster care system, the health care system, and the court system. In the informal infrastructure, there is a kind of hidden organization or networking of people and communities that you can't break down and define, but you know it's there and something is happening because of it. The term *infrastructure* attracted attention during the Vietnam War, when the U.S. was trying to figure out how a third world country could be so resilient against seemingly overwhelming U.S. military power. In the U.S. today, the police are daily confronted by the clandestine infrastructure that sustains illegal drug trafficking.

The drug infrastructure is tearing our communities apart just as other infrastructures are holding it together. There are extended family and friendship infrastructures that enable children to be clothed, fed, loved, and sent to school when the welfare check doesn't come or the working single parent gets sick and loses her job. Grandmothers, neighbors, and other people the public never notice step in and life goes on.

A major innovation in human services would be to find ways to bridge the formal public child welfare and other service infrastructures and the relatively invisible, informal extended family and neighborhood infrastructures that show up in response to need and then move out of sight. Regrettably, the current rescue-oriented social service system, which measures itself by units of service delivered rather than outcomes, is so compartmentalized that it is like a dinosaur in an age that requires instant communication and teamwork. A shift to a different paradigm is urgently needed to maximize the diminishing public funding and do the in-depth work necessary if we are ever to roll away the barriers and unbind the multitudes of overburdened families and children in the zone of persistent poverty.

AN ALTERNATIVE SYSTEM

What would an alternative foster care system look like, one shaped by a vision of individual, family, and community capacity-building rather than reaction to pain? People who think with the filter of a remedial or pain-driven orientation will find the question confusing. What can be more important or motivating than pain? The answer is that pain, like fear, is a short-lived motivation. It impels people to back away from something. Once the pain or fear is alleviated, pain-driven motivation is gone. Aspiration, or love-driven motivation, moves toward something. It is inherently generative and creative and sustainable provided its circuits stay open.

It is difficult to get a hearing where there is almost total fixation on the current system as the only option. The challenge is to frame an alternative that holds promise for getting on another track. The Casey Foundation Family to Family Initiative and the "Patch" program being developed in Iowa are promoting at a state level the kind of alternative neighborhood family service/foster care model we are speaking about in D.C. These models are beginning to demonstrate that:

- Social services can be improved in quality, accessibility and measurable outcomes through a neighborhood strategy at no greater financial cost than the current system.

- The development of neighborhood-based teams provides for a localized, flexible, proactive response to a continuum of needs, increases coordination, reduces duplication and fragmentation, supports and energizes informal helping networks, and empowers neighborhoods by engaging them in decision-making about services and priorities.

- A neighborhood strategy allows experimentation toward the decategorization and merging of child welfare funding streams, which could lead to generalizing this approach on a citywide and statewide scale.

- Neighborhood-based teams serve a limited geographical area, providing a shared neighborhood entry point to a wide array of services. Such teams can integrate workers at different levels of skill and specialization, including ancillary and volunteer workers.

LIVING SYSTEMS

It is the inevitable tendency of closed systems to wear down, to give off energy that does not recycle until the system can produce nothing more, and simply holds onto its space. Finally, permission is granted in some way to pronounce that death has occurred and to bury the corpse.

Quantum physics tells us that energy develops through connectedness and dissipates in isolation. Living systems are partners with the environment. Margaret Wheatley says that open systems have the possibility of continuously importing free energy from the environment and exporting entropy. They don't react quietly as their energy dissipates. They don't seek equilibrium, but quite the opposite. Open systems tolerate non-equilibrium, which keeps them off balance so that they can change and grow. They exchange actively with their world, using what is there for their own renewal.[2]

EMPOWERMENT

Both liberals and conservatives have used the term *empowerment* to articulate their social goals. It is interesting that this term was coined by the political left at the turn of the century and revived by the political right in the 1980s. When the political left started using the term in the early 1900s they were thinking of the inclusion of labor and minorities in political power. Political power in that era was dominated by the landholding class. Blue collar labor could not get an equal hearing in the press or legislative bodies. Being empowered meant becoming a participant and having influence on how resources controlled by the political process were divided. Empowering powerless groups meant organizing and enabling them to speak out, assert their rights, and get a place at the table.

The political right resurrected the term in the 1980s to define their goal for reform of the welfare system—improved functioning of individuals, elevation of self-esteem, and the economic betterment of the poor through development of skills and recovery of the work ethic. According to conservatives, all American citizens already have the right to vote. What holds them back is not political exclusion but failure to seize opportunities. So provide incentives, such as paying children to read books until reading becomes a habit.

Another working definition of empowerment is to support another person or group until they *experience* (i.e., "get") the role for which they are accountable as enlivening rather than draining.[3] A living system is one which empowers the people who work within it as well as its customers and clients.

A FUTURE OF INCLUSION

The challenge before us is to evolve toward a social vision that enables those at the bottom of the economic scale to become self-determining and be acknowledged as contributing citizens. How do we shift from our present mixture of containment and Social Darwinism toward a future of social and economic inclusion? In Chapter Eleven, I suggested the possibility of shifting from an acquisition- or possession-driven economy to a use- or experience-driven economy. The generative question is: What can the poor sell that other poor people, as well as the comfortable, are ready to buy? What examples of economic and social initiative, if they caught on, could start an evolutionary shift toward greater exchange among the poor and between the poor and the comfortable? What ideas for expansion of exchange could be seeded by individuals and groups at the local level, with or without government support?

CONSERVATIVE AND LIBERAL RESPONSES

The traditional conservative says that the market will take care of the problem, provided we allow the market to work as it can under limited government and low taxes. The traditional liberal says it can happen if we wrest control of the country from the greedy military-industrial-Wall Street complex, shift to a planned economy with a guaranteed minimum income, and establish decent, affordable housing, medical care, and quality education as a matter of right enforceable by the courts.

THE GENERATIVE ORIENTATION

Generative thinking says that we do not have to settle for what is, nor wait for a majority consensus to legislate all the ways the poor need to be included. What we can do is seed *living systems*. A living system is self-generating. An example is a classroom in which students have become responsible for their own learning to the point where the teacher can shift from controlling the learning process to coaching students in identifying and accomplishing their own learning objectives.

To see or amplify living systems we have to recognize when existing systems have broken down or reached their limit; that is, when they either no longer function or they require more investment than they justify in social benefit. Then comes the critical choice of pulling back resources from the existing system (or way of doing things) even before it breaks down or reaches its limit, to invest in experimentation. Can we tolerate a higher degree of disequilibrium while we experiment to find out what processes really help the poor for the long haul?

THE LAZARUS STORY:
A SEED OF NEW CONSCIOUSNESS

We have discussed a new social vision, one of high-level participation in opportunity and responsibility by people of diverse incomes, races, genders, traditions, and ages. We cannot talk about this vision as experts. It is beyond our experience, but it is compelling because it emerges from our deepest aspirations for the good life. Can we allow ourselves to think this way?

I see this question at the heart of the Lazarus story around which I have framed this book. In the story, Lazarus' sisters and neighbors go to the tomb to weep. That is all they know to do. One neighbor, no doubt, asked, "Why did he have to die before his time?" Others, just as likely, would be quick to answer, "He's better off now" or "His dying was the will of God."

This is not Jesus' response. When he sees everyone weeping, Jesus groans to the point of tears. The Greek word describing Jesus' response denotes anger rather than sorrow. The neighbors mistakenly interpret Jesus' weeping as loving resignation. As the story unfolds, it becomes clear that instead, Jesus is reacting to their unawareness of new possibility.

Jesus believes that God is present and active. Jesus believes that God is about to make a statement in the human arena: that God is on the side of life. This opportunity cannot be missed. To embrace the opportunity is to enter the process of transformation, to engage with the power of Spirit.

In the Lazarus story, Jesus calls the community into action. All, including Jesus, move into territory where they have never been before. The steps Jesus takes are as much a journey of faith on his part as they are on the part of those who follow his direction. "Roll away the stone." "Lazarus, come forth." "Unbind him, let him go." Jesus weaves together the energies within himself and the latent energies of the community and the victim as a response to his consciousness of grace in the situation. What occurs, the re-emergence of Lazarus into life, is called a miracle because it lies outside the realm of human rationality.

When Jesus arrives at the sealed tomb of Lazarus, the stage is set for a continuation of the original creation story, when God created the world in stages, first the firmament, then light, and so on. From a strictly human perspective, life is over for Lazarus. Death, nonbeing, has had the last word. Jesus embodies a counter-message. Where the empowering word is active, there is a different balance of power. God continues to be Creator, and God is not finished with this world. The raising of Lazarus is a sign of the radical newness of God's vision for the world. The timing of the breakthough of newness is part of God's freedom.

The change that Jesus sets in motion recalls the vision of Exodus 3, where God says to Moses, "I have seen the affliction of my people who are in Egypt, and heard their cry because of their taskmasters; I know their sufferings, and I have come down to deliver them out of the hand of the Egyptians, and to bring them out of that land to a good and broad land, a land flowing with milk and honey..." Lazarus will awaken.

GOD ON THE SIDE OF THE POOR

For those of us who aspire to put our religious beliefs into action, we ask, "How can we conceive of God leading us in working with the economic, political, social, and personal forces at play in human affairs today?" How might the inclusive process Jesus models in the raising of Lazarus translate for the equally incredible task today of liberating the persistently poor? Whether we are orthodox or heterodox, what would stir in us humble trust that we are joined by power and love far greater than ourselves in a common struggle for a better world? What would inspire the courage to act out this trust?

In Chapters Nine through Eleven, I described the basic premise of the living systems paradigm: the world is an evolving organism, sometimes regressing and sometimes evolving toward betterment. When it evolves forward, it includes human inventiveness; and discovery and inventiveness often come with breakdown of the familiar.

One response to breakdown is containment. But choosing a future of containment ensures that the poor will be denied the ability to participate in exchange. This is a form of resistance to Spirit. On the other hand, participation with an open mind and heart toward those whose interests may seem different from ours, even those whom we perceive as threats to us, leads to the possibility of newness. And newness derives from greater differentiation of individuals and cultures and authentic integration through honest exchange. The flow of evolution is like this, and facing the fact of evolution, we only have two choices: (1) to defend against it until its force builds, like a flood, to break through our dikes, or (2) to accept it and work with it.

From a Judaeo-Christian perspective, God cannot be equated with any natural process, including evolution. However, if we think of evolution as transformation toward greater complexity and richness, it may be that this is a primary way God is relating to the world in our time. It may be that God in the form of Spirit is participating in our modern process of expanding consciousness of the uniqueness of men and women, old and young, black, white, yellow, and brown, and of the world's incredibly diverse cultures. The more each piece of the whole comes into its own, the more it has to contribute to the expanding richness of the whole. I believe the process of differentiation into unique parts, then integration through the exchange of the unique gifts of the differentiated parts, is where reality is moving. This is where I think the train is headed. All of us therefore have arenas to work in, and somehow our separate and scattered efforts, when aligned with our deepest aspirations, are part of a mysterious convergence.

All of this leads to one incredible point. Appearances to the contrary, the long view of evolution suggests that God really is on the side of the poor because of the inherent worth of all creatures. And their economic, social, political, and individual inclusion means more abundant life for all. By being on the side of the poor, God is on the side of all, because the inclusion of all is the future. And by actively choosing this future, whether we know it or not, we are surrendering to God.

The Lazarus story is not so farfetched after all. Its simple directions point the way. Yes, roll away the stones. Come forth both poor and comfortable. Unbind us, let us all go! Amen.

SAVING AMERICA'S CHILDREN

Endnotes

CHAPTER ONE

1. Joan Paddock Maxwell, *No Easy Answers* (Greater Washington Research Center, December, 1985), pp. 12f.

2. <u>Ibid.</u>

3. Michael Barone, editorial, *The Washington Post,* February 10, 1986.

CHAPTER THREE

1. Shirley Brice Heath, *Way With Words* (Cambridge University Press, 1983).

2. <u>Ibid.,</u> p.2

3. <u>Ibid.</u>

ENDNOTES _____ 261

4. Landmark Education Corporation developed and utilizes this theme of "putting the past in the past" in its excellent training courses, particularly the Forum and Advanced Course. For further information, write Landmark Education, 6295 Edsall Road, Alexandria, VA 22310.

5. Testimony before the Council of the District of Columbia Committee on Housing hearing, February 18, 1993, by Lynn E. Cunningham, Esq. and Dr. Dorothy Remy.

CHAPTER FOUR

1. George Bernanos, *The Diary of a Country Priest* (Image Books, 1954), p.1.

2. This diagram draws upon the description of vicious and liberating circles in Jurgen Moltmann, *The Crucified God* (Harper and Row, 1974), pp. 329-335.

3. Ibid., p. 294.

4. Testimony of a participant at a Landmark Education training event. Distributed as a handout.

5. Elizabeth O'Connor, *Journey Inward, Journey Outward* (Harper and Row, 1968).

6. Deuteronomy 24:19-22.

CHAPTER SEVEN

1. Paulo Freire, *Pedagogy of the Oppressed* (Herder and Herder, 1990), p. 14.

CHAPTER NINE

1. A Landmark Education Corporation training theme.

2. Adapted from training seminar, "Working from the Heart," Jackie McMakin, McLean, Va.

3. Lisbeth B. Schorr, *Within Our Reach* (Doubleday, 1988), p. xvii.

4. Drexel Sprecher, seminar "The Future of Leadership" and private conversations. For further information write Drexel Sprecher, 133 Kearny Street, Suite 300, San Francisco, CA 94108.

5. James Pinkerton, former Deputy Assistant to the President for Policy Planning, from remarks to the Illinois New Paradigm Society, September 16, 1991. Reprinted in Youth Policy, November/December 1991, Volume 14, Number 8, pp. 21-22.

6. Joanna Macy, Noetic Sciences Bulletin, Winter 1994-5, p. 2.

CHAPTER TEN

1. Margaret Wheatley, *Leadership and the New Science* (Berrett-Koehler, 1994), p. 42.

2. Ibid., p. 6.

3. Ibid., p. 8.

CHAPTER ELEVEN

1. Conversation with Drexel Sprecher.

2. John E. Schwarz, *America's Hidden Success* (W.W. Norton and Co., 1983), pp. 34ff.

CHAPTER TWELVE

1. John Kretzmann and John McKnight, *Building Communities from the Inside Out* (Center for Urban Affairs and Policy Research, Evanston, IL. 60208, 1993), p. 2.

2. Wheatley, op. cit., p. 8.

3. Conversation with Drexel Sprecher.